TOYS FOR A LIFETIME

First published in the United States of America in 1999
by UNIVERSE PUBLISHING
A Division of Rizzoli International Publications, Inc.
300 Park Avenue South
New York, NY 10010

99 00 01 02 / 10 9 8 7 6 5 4 3 2 1

Designed by 27.12 design, ltd.

Printed in England

Library of Congress Cataloging-in-Publication Data
Auerbach, Stevanne.
F.A.O. Schwarz toys for a lifetime: enhancing childhood through
play / by Stevanne "Dr. Toy" Auerbach.
p. cm.
ISBN 0-7893-0355-8 hc
1. Toys--United States. 2. Toys--United States--Psychological
aspects. 3. F.A.O. Schwarz (Firm) I. Title.
TS2301.T7A777 1999
790.1'33--dc21
99-23711
CIP

F·A·O Schwarz

TOYS FOR A LIFETIME

Enhancing Childhood Through Play

BY STEVANNE "DR. TOY" AUERBACH, PH. D.

PHOTOGRAPHS BY BEN ASEN

UNIVERSE

A Byron Preiss Book

Contents

INTRODUCTION
vi

STARTING OUT: TOYS FOR THE FIRST YEARS OF LIFE
1

Surrounding your baby with sensations, delight, and wonder

BUILDING BLOCKS: STEPPING STONES TO CREATIVITY
15

Helping little construction workers build the world of their dreams

ARTS AND CRAFTS: TERRIFIC TOOLS FOR THE ARTIST-TO-BE
29

Unleashing your child's imagination

**DOLLS, STUFFED ANIMALS, AND ACTION FIGURES:
COMPANIONS TO DISCOVERY AND FRIENDS FOR LIFE**
43

Selecting playmates for your child to cherish

GAMES: CHALLENGE AND COMPETITION FOR ALL AGES
61

Teaching your child to play the way to success

TRANSPORTATION TOYS: PLANES, TRAINS, AND AUTOMOBILES
75

Providing a crash course in excitement and adventure for the child on the go

SILLY FUN: EDUCATED NONSENSE
89

Keeping your child amused for hours

OUTDOOR TOYS: PATHWAYS TO ATHLETIC ADVENTURE
103

Encouraging physical skills, competition, and teamwork

FUTURE TOYS: TRENDS TOWARD TECH
119

Revolutionizing the way children learn and play with interactive toys

ABOUT DR. TOY
134

ACKNOWLEDGMENTS
135

CREDITS
136

INTRODUCTION

When I was a young child, the very best days began with putting on my patent-leather shoes and special Sunday dress and going with my parents to the FAO Schwarz store in Manhattan. While the trip on the subway from Queens was long, it was always the beginning of lasting memories. I can still vividly recall one day when I went looking for a Shirley Temple doll.

Today, children still treasure that special trip and enjoy the magic of an FAO Schwarz store. Toys are, after all, magical; they are the building blocks of childhood. FAO Schwarz has always been the pinnacle, the premier toy showcase, the great pyramid of play, the granddaddy of them all, a place of unique charisma, pizzazz, and cachet. It is everything a toy store should be, and more.

Throughout its extensive history, FAO's careful, well-orchestrated mix of products has always generated a special excitement. The store provides many opportunities to touch, play with, and feel products. This tactile relationship is very important to young children. Many products are demonstrated by store personnel to help show parents, grandparents, and others how a toy works. After all, not everything can be fully understood just by reading the box (think Silly Putty).

For this reason and more, writing this book has been a particularly special opportunity for me. I have admired the store for its dedicated service, remarkable history, high standards, and longevity. The history contained in this book reflects the close relationship of the store to the history of toys in America.

Toys for a Lifetime features a select group of classic toys. Our definition of *classic* means that the toy has proved over time to be safe, consistently popular, well-designed, practical, and a good value for the money. But most of all, to be a classic, a toy must encourage a child's involvement. For example, anyone who has ever tried a hula hoop knows that it's a great challenge to swirl that colorful plastic hoop.

Classic toys take you back to your childhood. Just by closing your eyes, you can instantly recall the joy. Can you remember the first time you played with a yo-yo, Etch-A-Sketch, or Mr. Potato Head? These toys are enduring, "child-powered," and fun. They have entertained and enriched the lives of children and adults for years. Fortunately for our children, many of these classics are constantly in demand and, therefore, always available.

The toys that have been included in this book encompass the entire range in the industry— everything from dolls to transportation toys, from low-tech to high-tech, from babies to older children. I've highlighted the history of selected toy companies to give you some sense of the tradition of the industry over many generations.

In *Toys for a Lifetime*, you'll learn which toys are appropriate for children of any age. You'll enjoy the excitement of finding just the right toys or games for the children in your life—maybe a cuddly teddy bear or an undulating Slinky. There are classic toys to match every interest.

Also included is a wide variety of people's reflections of their toys and how their experiences influenced their future. I am firmly convinced that our early play dramatically affects our outlook and behavior as adults. Demonstrating the importance of play is really the overall goal of this book. It is my hope that this book will guide parents toward expanding their appreciation of the importance of play for their children. Playing reduces stress, improves life, and increases creativity. Who doesn't want that?

And appreciating the importance of play means there will be smiles as big as mine when I received my Shirley Temple doll, all those years ago.

— STEVANNE "DR. TOY" AUERBACH

STARTING OUT

TOYS FOR THE FIRST YEARS OF LIFE

Each baby's personality is unique, but all babies develop their senses of sight, sound, smell, and touch the same way. They look and listen; they relate to people and objects. Thus, the first three years are crucial for a child's total development. The more conflict-free and stimulating the environment, the better it is for the baby.

By encouraging investigation of the world through play and the appropriate toys, you help your child progress confidently. For example, when your daughter pulls herself up to stand, she learns that the object she is holding on to is stable and permanent. Or when your son plays peekaboo, he learns that objects exist even when he can't see them. When he drops and picks up a rattle, he begins to understand cause-and-effect relationships.

A baby imitates behavior; he will often laugh when you laugh, play when you play, and soak up learning every step of the way. If you enjoy interacting with toys, your child will follow suit. Helping children to use their imagination will open them up to all of the wonderful, daily opportunities for play.

When babies are first born, they can only see objects about seven to ten inches away but soon are able to track such objects with their eyes. New-borns' attention span lasts about ten seconds for a face and about five seconds for a design. Soon your baby will connect seeing you walk across the room with hearing footsteps, essentially imagining you when she hears the sound. You can feed your baby's imagination with new sights, varieties of light, and patterns.

A baby's color perception does not fully develop until he is about four to six months old. Until then, babies are fascinated by color extremes like white, black, or red, and wild patterns of circles, stripes, and checks.

Some companies—such as Learning Curve, Manhattan Baby, Wimmer-Ferguson, and Eden—have created plush toys and mobiles incorporating these stimuli.

Sound is also incredibly important to learning. Studies prove that babies can hear in utero, and infants are able to recognize their parents' voices very shortly after birth. When babies coo and make sounds, be sure to respond and coo at them to encourage both verbal communication and language. Some toys, such as music boxes and tape recorders, can increase your baby's awareness to sound. Toys that make music and other appealing sounds are good investments throughout childhood.

Babies are sensitive to touch and determine information through this sense. As they absorb new sensory experiences, babies learn to connect what objects look like with how they feel. By providing lots of tactile sensations, you're activating the part of the mind where imagination develops.

Babies need to be cuddled, reassured, and securely held. When infants feel comfortable in their surroundings, they will feel more confident about exploring. When babies are very small, they don't have command over their movements but will experiment by raising their heads and moving their arms and legs. Gradually these movements will become more and more controlled. By the third month, babies have a much wider range of motion; they grab your glasses and their toes and reach out to touch things. Soon they are kicking the toys hanging above them.

As babies go from exploring their own hands to exploring toys, they become excited, adventurous, and increasingly fascinated with new objects. You can help by finding your child something novel and unusual to hold on to.

At six months, babies begin to crawl and stand. They enjoy looking in mirrors, talking to themselves, being carried around to explore the world, and picking up objects and dropping them. From five to seven months, babies also enjoy toys they can feel, bite, and suck. Babies put anything they can get their hands around into their mouths, so be sure that their toys are clean and too large to swallow.

The toys discussed here are appropriate for children up to two years old, who especially need stimulation and variety to learn.

ACTIVITY GYM

BABY'S MOBILE GOES INTERACTIVE

Up to 10 months

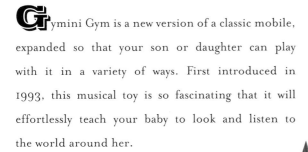

Gymini Gym is a new version of a classic mobile, expanded so that your son or daughter can play with it in a variety of ways. First introduced in 1993, this musical toy is so fascinating that it will effortlessly teach your baby to look and listen to the world around her.

The structure of the Gymini Gym is based on colorful arches designed so soft toys can be attached. Because it is padded, your baby can lie on top of the mat and play on it or roll over and around and still be secure. This toy is good for infant motor-skill development because it encourages a baby to respond to the intriguing environment it offers. There is nothing quite like watching those tantalizingly close colors and shapes as they dance in the breeze.

Your new baby can play with this toy at home or during travel, because the Gymini Gym is easy to store and easy to set up. Everything is removable and simple to clean. Accessories include extra rings for attaching additional toys, a plastic rattle that makes soft sounds, and a mirror, which babies will look at endlessly. All this looking and moving and listening provide a good foundation for early self-esteem and face recognition.

A variety of Gyminis are available, with different themes and different colors (black and white, and the primary colors). If you want to bring this safe play area outdoors, Tiny Love also makes a canopy. Other excellent products in this line for the growing child include the 1-2-3 Discovery Line, crib and stroller accessories, and puppets.

Gymini is a *true* original and the leading activity gym on the market today. Tiny Love was founded in Israel by a retailer who saw a need for improved soft toys and more adventurous toys for very young babies. The combination of safe toys and challenging activities in a protective environment provides the building blocks from which children can grow.

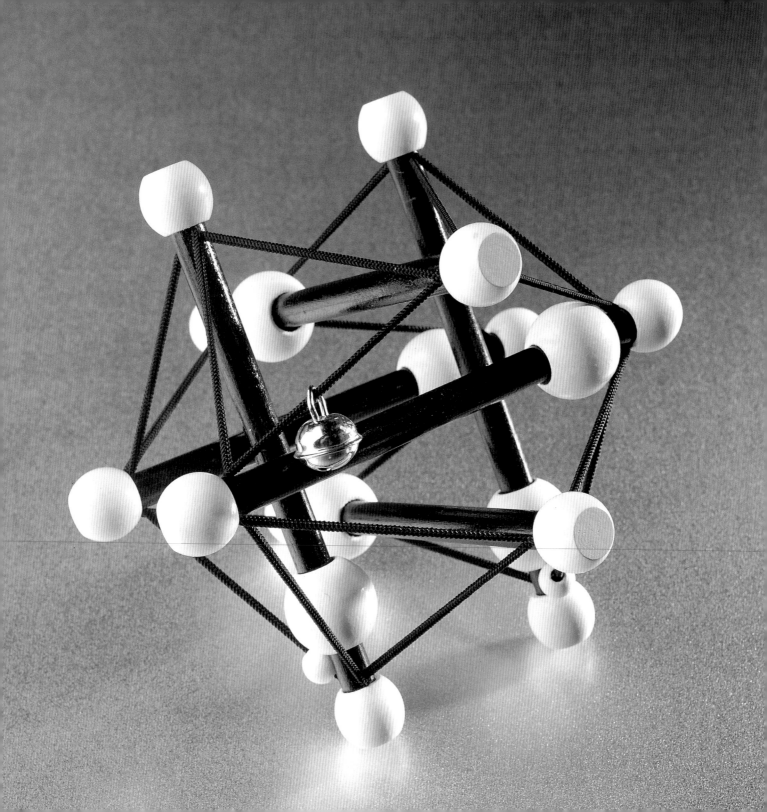

SKWISH

GREAT FOR GRASPING AND HOLDING

6–24 months

Skwish is the ultimate baby toy, with bright colors, sliding beads, and a jingling bell. This collapsible toy offers hours of fun for babies who have just discovered that their hands are made for grasping, shaking, squeezing, and rattling whatever is in reach. Made from solid, smooth birch wood and nontoxic paint, Skwish can handle being roughly treated.

The simple act of passing Skwish back and forth will give a baby a lot of pleasure. Successfully grasping an object is important, so this toy is ideal, because it is so easy to hold. Toys that are too difficult for a baby to hold can lead to failure and frustration. A great crib or carriage toy, Skwish is well-suited for either home or travel. It can easily become a daily favorite to be treasured for a long time.

Skwish was designed by Tom Flemons while he was studying Buckminster Fuller's "tensegrity" structures—models that show coexistent tension and compression and are comprised of a complex network of triangles that form a roughly spherical shape. Flemons developed Skwish by scaling down his larger version to fit a baby's grasp. Founded in 1985, Pappa Geppetto's Toys began as a small manufacturer of wooden toys and gifts. Currently the company works with independent designers around the world to develop new and unusual toys.

Baby Shower Gift Ideas

1. Bath toys
2. Cloth blocks
3. Crib gym
4. Mirror
5. Mobile
6. Music box
7. Rattle
8. Stuffed animals
9. Tape recorder and tapes
10. Teether

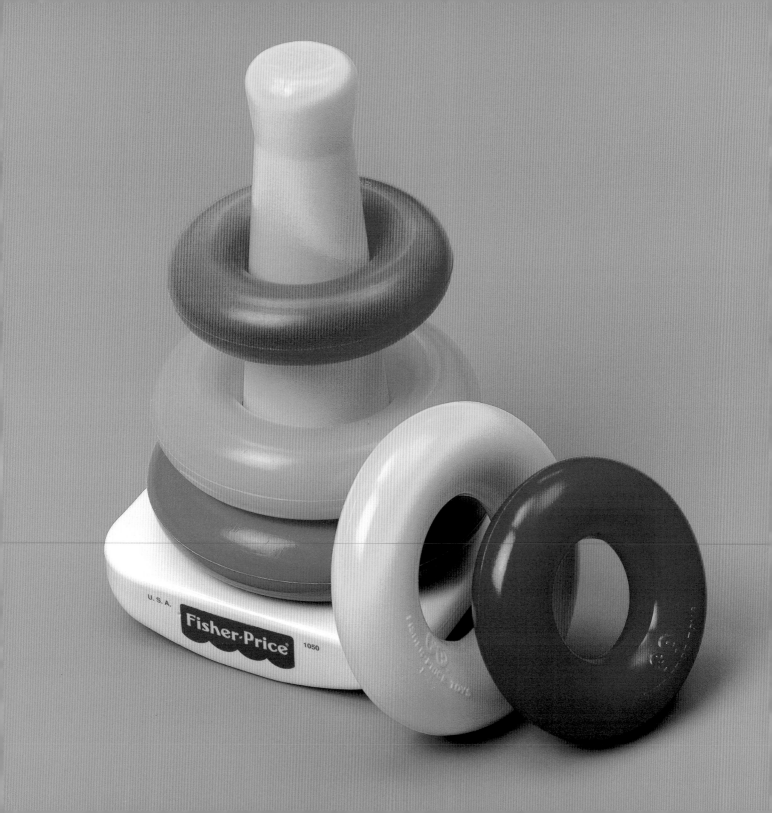

STACKING RINGS

A TEETHING TOOL THAT TEACHES, TOO

(*Fisher-Price*, 1940), 6–36 months

tacking rings are a true basic, traditional toy. There are five brightly colored rings on a stack, and babies can place the rings on the stack in whatever order they wish. There are many different color and stacking combinations, and that's a lot of eye-hand coordination practice!

Later, babies can use the rings to identify colors and practice counting when placing them on the stack. Taking them off and stacking them upside down is also fun. An additional bonus is that the rings make great teethers. Children usually play with their rings for a long time. Stacking rings are a staple— a versatile and safe toy to captivate active babies and toddlers.

The Rock-A-Stack is a rounded variation of the basic platform that allows your child to initiate an additional movement. Rock-A-Stack comes in both a standard and a giant size.

The manufacturer, Fisher-Price, is a leader in infant and preschool toys. The company was founded in 1930 in East Aurora, New York, by Herman Fisher, Irving Price, and Helen Schelle. In 1993, a merger made Fisher-Price a subsidiary of Mattel. Fisher-Price focuses on three areas— infant, preschool, and juvenile products. Decorated in primary colors, Fisher-Price toys are easy to clean, fun to use, and well designed for the intended age group.

TOY SAFETY TIPS FOR BABIES

BE SURE PRODUCTS YOU SELECT FOR YOUR BABY HAVE:

Nontoxic paint, No sharp edges, No loose ties, No small pieces, No loose pieces, Are hypoallergenic, Guaranteed safety-tested

GAZOOBO

A TODDLER'S MENAGERIE OF COLORS AND SHAPES

18 months—4 years

Gazoobo, a zoo-house shape sorter, is a classic all over the world. This wonderful busy box will help your baby learn colors, shapes, and sizes and how to match the shapes with the different doors.

Gazoobo has six animals and shapes, which slot into the color-coded doors that correspond to each animal. There are colored keys for each door, including a passkey that opens up all the doors so your child can retrieve the shapes. The plastic shapes are durable, and, as an additional activity, children can place the shapes on top of paper and then draw the outline. Also, there are stickers for each animal shape and a good, pull-out carrying handle. This product is perfect for the young child working on eye-hand coordination.

For more than forty years, Chicco has gained the trust of parents in more than seventy-five countries with a comprehensive line of products created exclusively to make a baby's life a little happier and his parents' life a little easier. Headquartered in Como, Italy, Chicco was founded by Pietro Catelli and his sons. Working together, they determined the names Lycia and Chicco for the product lines. The latter has become synonymous with infant care, as the children are the focus of the family.

The family's personal touch and human involvement is evident in all Chicco products. Chicco is committed to an ongoing, intensive research-and-development program. Besides technicians and designers, Chicco enlists the expertise of pediatricians and specialists in every aspect of child care. This outstanding Italian company produces high-quality toys and children's products. Chicco is constantly improving their classic toys and offering new designs to make products safer and playtime even more fun.

10

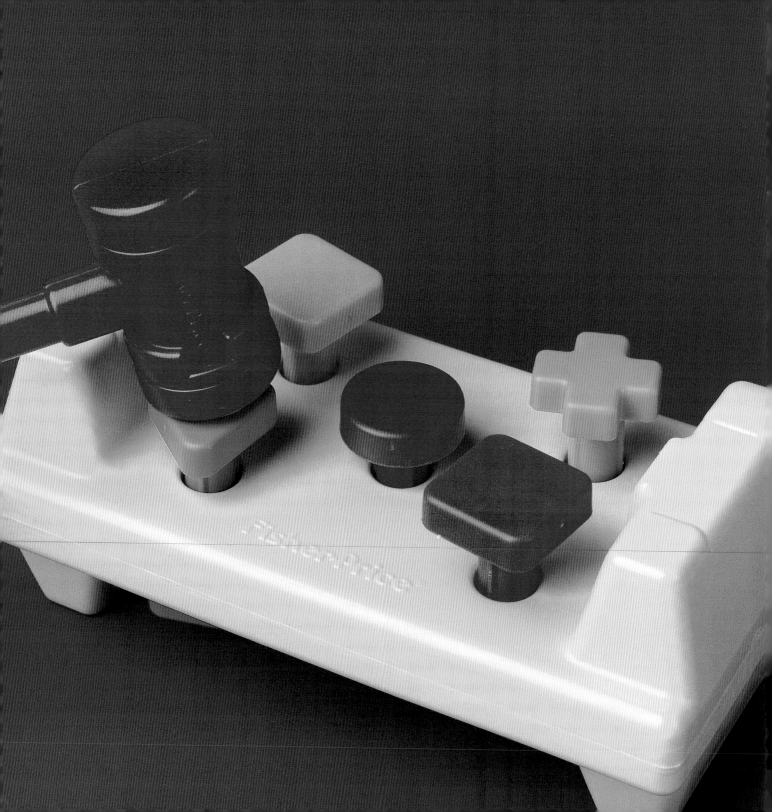

TAP AND TURN BENCH

AN ASPIRING CARPENTER'S FIRST TOOL SET

18 months–3 years

For years, kids have loved the pounding action of this workbench with colorful pegs trapped inside. This sturdy plastic toy is two-sided, so even small children can flip it over and continue pounding. (And they will, they will.)

Children like to use their arms. As soon as they can clench their fists, they can control the mallet. There is an entire repertoire of hammering techniques, and some children use them all. A child may hammer with one hand, use both hands together, or she may alternate, using one hand and then the other—any way to get the pegs hammered in.

When a child is using the Tap and Turn Bench, parents should say things like

FAO SCHWARZ, 1963

"bang, bang" or clap their hands to encourage their child to make sounds too. It's wonderful what you can do with the hammer, without damaging furniture or other things. It is fun to pound and be noisy. This toy is really good for helping children develop a clear and firm sense of their physical self as well as eye-hand coordination. It also gives children an acceptable and safe way to express their feelings.

Most children go back to this product from time to time throughout their early childhood. They really enjoy using it, probably because they can see something happening when they pound. Accomplishment always feeds practice and competency.

CORN POPPER

A PERFECT PUSH-PULL FOR NEW WALKERS

9 months–3 years

Babies begin pulling themselves up to a standing position after six months. They will need help learning to keep their balance. Soon they will be walking around and seeing how far they can get on their own. Before your baby reaches this stage, take time to "babyproof" your house. Once babies even start crawling, they are able to get into everything and must be watched carefully.

When babies are able to walk, they enjoy pulling toys with strings or pushing a push-pull toy ahead of them. Instead of holding on to someone's hand, a push-pull toy will allow a small child a bit of independence. That makes the push-pull Corn Popper toy an ideal choice. Babies will enjoy the toy's soft popping sounds, and this pleasure will compensate for their lapses in balance. For new walkers, push-pull toys like the Corn Popper also add the incentive of fun to confidence-building mastery. The multicolored balls pop inside the clear bubble as a response to the child's walking. The popping fascinates children, and they keep walking to keep hearing the pops. The toy has a durable handle, so it will hold up to all that travel. As your child's walking improves, the Corn Popper will remain a favorite push-pull plaything. The Corn Popper is another classic toy from Fisher-Price. This sort of sturdy and carefully designed toy works with your child's growth patterns and makes learning and practice painless and carefree.

POP-POP SWEEPER
FAO SCHWARZ, 1968

BUILDING BLOCKS

STEPPING STONES TO CREATIVITY

Simple building play sets and building blocks provide a very important experience for children. From the earliest soft terry-cloth or foam blocks to the most high-tech interactive set, all present a tangible challenge to children: "If I put this part here, will it work?" While playing with these construction toys, children are forced to think about fit, angles, gravity, size and space relationships, and cause-and-effect.

Open-ended sets, or those not designed to create a specific thing, allow children to create something completely new with their own imaginations. Or the goal can be more focused, to create a pictured end result, like a realistic model of an airplane or car.

With any type of set, children get plenty of stimulation for their eye-hand and

The Mysto ERECTOR

small-muscle coordination. They begin to see how to use space appropriately as they assemble their structures. Building also enhances children's ability to connect what they see with what they can do. Their initiative to build helps them develop greater self-esteem and independence. An added bonus to construction toys is that children increase their language development and their social ability by cooperating on building structures together.

Many sets combine accessories with the blocks, including little people, cars, signs, animals, and other toys that enhance the sets' uses. Many times these specialized sets come as buildable cities, farms, airports, and stores. Besides the ones featured here, companies that make outstanding construction sets are Robotix, Rokenbok, Megablock, BRIO, NSI, and Primordial.

Many famous architects used blocks as children. The blocks helped them expand their creativity as they took on the roles of pint-size builders, engineers, and planners. Famous nineteenth-century

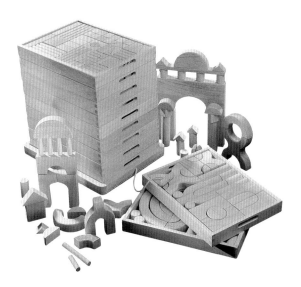

parents claim they can distinguish one set from another just by stepping on a piece in the dark. But no parents can complain about open-ended toys like blocks, because they help their children learn as they are exercising their creativity.

German educator Friedrich Froebel, known as the father of kindergarten, was actually trained as an architect. He spoke often of the importance of playing with blocks and construction materials. The blocks that he created, the Froebel blocks, developed into a basic set of materials that could be found in kindergartens throughout the world.

In the twentieth century, many sets have found a place on our floors and in our classrooms: Tinkertoys, Erector Sets, Lincoln Logs, Lego, Playmobil, Zoob, Toobers & Zots, Knex, to name a few. Many

ALPHABET BLOCKS

A-B-C, EASY AS 1-2-3

2–5 years

Children can learn the alphabet the old-fashioned way with these highly detailed, handcrafted wooden blocks. These 1.75-inch basswood blocks are brightly colored with child-safe inks, and the four sides of the twenty-seven blocks include four complete alphabets, three sets of numerals, and twenty-seven different animal pictures.

Based on a set made in 1879, these pint-size treasures will become your child's favorite for a variety of reasons. They are objects your child can hold on to and manipulate, they can be stacked, and they can be knocked down. These blocks can become whatever the child wants them to be. And, as they play with these blocks, children can't help but become more familiar with numbers, letters, colors, and animals.

Uncle Goose was founded by William Bultman, who reintroduced the classic, embossed ABC block in 1983, when he discovered that the blocks he had played with as a child were no longer available. His company was making classic wagons at the time, and he added the Uncle Goose alphabet blocks to the mix. Since then, he has passed the business on to his sons, Scott and Peter, who have kept the tradition alive.

· TOYS I REMEMBER ·

WHEN I WAS ABOUT FIVE OR SIX YEARS OLD, *my favorite plaything was one of the earliest and most basic construction toys—an Erector Set. I still remember fastening four little wheels to a flat metal base, thus building my very own wagon, which I spent hours pulling and pushing all around the floor. I also built tiny bridges, simple buildings, and my own private little army of figures.*

I've always felt that the basic, uncomplicated Erector Set somehow helped to nurture both my imagination and any feelings of creativity I might have had. —STAN LEE, **creator of** *Spiderman*

Lego: Big Bricks for Little Hands

- Carpenter Ole Kirk Christiansen founded the company in 1932 and originally created the bricks in wood. The name Lego is derived from Danish words *leg godt* meaning "play well." *Lego* also means "assemble" in Latin.

- Lego manufactures in Denmark, the United States, and other places. More than 189 billion plastic elements have been produced since 1949. The bricks are manufactured seven days a week, twenty-four hours a day. Lego toys are sold in more than 130 countries.

- The first Legoland park opened in 1968 in Billund, Denmark. A scale model of Mt. Rushmore at Legoland Billund is made from 1.5 million Lego bricks and was assembled by crane. Legoland, California, opened in March, 1999.

LEGO

BUILDING BLOCKS FOR EVERY AGE

3 months–16 years

In a child's hands, all versions of Lego bricks can easily be transformed into whatever he or she can imagine. These simple, studded bricks in primary colors can be put together or pulled apart to become a castle, a spaceship, a farm—the possibilities are endless. Enhancing a natural part of play, Lego bricks help children focus their attention and encourage creativity by enabling them to build, enjoy their construction, destroy it, and rebuild again. The role-playing and adventure play also trigger increased language and communication skills.

At whatever age children begin playing with Lego, the system—which includes Primo, Duplo, Lego, and Lego Technic—grows with them every step of the way. From age three months to two years, the large pieces of Primo are easy for the young child to hold and manipulate, and the set expands in difficulty as the child's eye-hand coordination improves. Primo provides blocks that are smooth, safe, and—with rattles, people figures, and other unique elements—sometimes even surprising.

Between the ages of eighteen months and five years, the child can use the Duplo set with pieces eight times the size of the standard Lego brick. Beyond the benefits derived from basic building, Duplo bricks also encourage language development.

The basic Lego sets are ideal for children ages three to twelve and are available in a "freestyle form" that allows your child to build castles as big as their dreams. There are also sets that take them into different environments, such as the prehistoric world of dinosaurs or the moon's craggy surface. These building and play-acting activities are perfect to enhance a child's mental and physical development, encourage self-confidence, and develop coordination.

From ages seven to sixteen, the more advanced system, Lego Technic, enables your child to build realistic models that offer additional excitement by providing motors that enable the product to move in different directions.

TINKERTOYS

LIMITLESS POSSIBILITIES FOR LIMITLESS IMAGINATIONS

18 months–7 years

Tinkertoys, one of the first popular building sets, have served as a tool of creativity for generations. Originally made of unpainted wood, this unique series of colorful sticks and bases with corresponding holes connects in a wide variety of ways, allowing for a slew of outlandish creations. Tinkertoys are admired not only by parents and educators, but also by architects and museums. Children can use Tinkertoys to create fanciful structures, amazing animals, and bizarre vehicles. The only limit is the child's imagination.

This architectural toy was the brainchild of Charles Pajeau, a stone mason, who was inspired when his children built structures by sticking pencils into empty spools of thread. After modifying the design to create a shorter, wheellike spool with a series of holes running around the edge, Pajeau and his partner, Robert Petit, were ready to meet with toy manufacturers. The response was decidedly underwhelming at the New York Toy Fair of 1914. To create interest, Pajeau and Petit set up an elaborate display in the pharmacy of Grand Central Station. Within days, the display generated thousands of sales. Millions of Tinkertoys have been sold every year since.

· TOYS I REMEMBER ·

Almost every toy I enjoyed was somehow involved with building operations. When I was a little boy my favorite toy was my Erector Set. I enjoyed it because it had so many complex parts and I could build things with it. We had a three-story house and I built an elevator that could go from downstairs to the third floor. This elevator was big enough to transport my morning orange juice from the kitchen to me in my bedroom on the third floor. Building and operating continue to be my passion: it is what I do to this day.
—CHARLES CONRAD, JR., NASA astronaut

PLAYMOBIL

FABULOUS FANTASY WORLDS

18 months–7 years

For twenty years, Playmobil's philosophy has been that creative toys play an important role in learning. Their playsets, filled with architectural elements and figures, are designed to develop young minds by appealing to children's fantasies and imaginations. Perfectly designed for little hands and growing minds, the pieces are durably crafted, with bright colors, rounded edges, and inviting themes. And as an added bonus to parents, each set is fully washable.

Playmobil has created over 275 different sets, all scaled to work together. Thematic lines include elaborate dollhouses with scaled room sets; System X, which features such detailed constructions as a city house, a police station, and a bike shop; and a radio-controlled train set that can be taken outside and works from thirty feet away. But even the basic sets—such as the farm,

the neighborhood, the medieval kingdom, and the ocean world—include everything needed for great fun and countless hours of playtime.

When he was young, Playmobil creator Hans Beck made toys for his siblings. As he grew older, he learned cabinetmaking and later went on to design toys. In 1971 he created his first Playmobil system. Playmobil, now a subsidiary of the 150-year-old German manufacturer Geobrabrandstatter, is a worldwide favorite.

LINCOLN LOGS

YOUNG BUILDERS GO WEST

4–8 years

This classic construction toy has been a favorite for generations. Over the years, millions of children have settled the Wild West, building pioneer cabins, forts, towns, and ranches with Lincoln Logs. All Lincoln Log sets feature easy-fitting, durable, real wood and plastic pieces so kids can build lots of imaginative structures again and again. The individual sets can be combined to create larger scenes.

The inventor, architect John Lloyd

FAO SCHWARZ, 1943

Wright, knew what these logs really looked like. His idea for the toy was inspired by a technique of interlocking beams used by his father, Frank Lloyd Wright, in his design for Tokyo's Imperial Hotel in 1916.

Named for Abraham Lincoln (who was born in a log cabin), the original product was constructed of redwood. Many other toy companies soon capitalized on the success of Lincoln Logs, flooding the market with similar designs.

TOY SAFETY CHECKLIST

1. Pay attention to age recommendations and safety messages on toy packaging.
2. Consider the age of younger children when buying toys for older children in the family.
3. For children under the age of three, avoid toys with small parts that could be swallowed or inhaled and those with rough edges.
4. Make sure that all elements of the toy are securely fastened and cannot be pulled or bitten off.
5. If selecting a toy with arrows and darts, be certain the tips are blunt and securely fastened to the shafts.
6. All soft and cloth toys should be machine/surface washable.
7. All electrical toys should be approved by Underwriters Laboratory (UL).

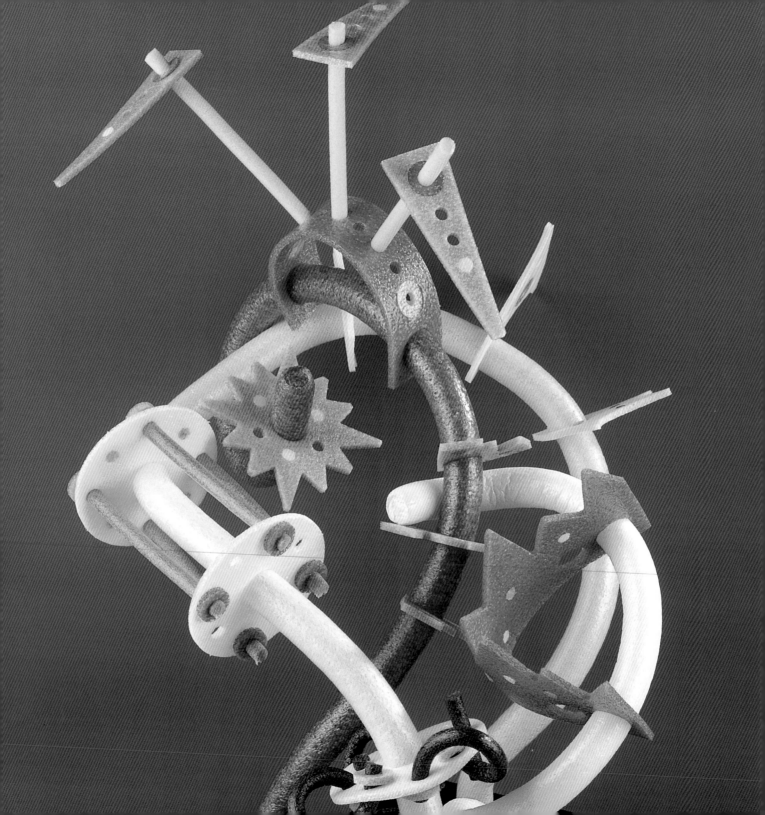

FLEXIBLE CONSTRUCTION SET

CREATING CRAZY CONSTRUCTIONS

5–8 years

Flexible, holdable, and infinitely moldable, Toobers & Zots inspires hours of open-ended, creative fun. Toobers—long, bendable foam tubes—hold their shape and are lightweight and fun to use. Colorful Zots are an assortment of stars, circles, squares, triangles, donuts, crowns, and other shapes that connect with Toobers like beads on a string. This large-scale flexible construction set is made of colorful foam, with soft aluminum cores similar to giant pipe cleaners.

Where did this wildly weird toy come from? From a kitchen table in Cambridge, Massachusetts, where three old friends—all fathers with young children—decided to design and manufacture highly interactive educational toys. Andy Farrar, Rustam Booz, and Arthur Ganson formed a company called Hands On Toys and spent many months brainstorming and designing.

In 1994, the grand idea for Toobers & Zots came to Arthur Ganson, an artist, kinetic sculptor, and artist-in-residence at MIT. In August 1994, the company tried the toy at the New York Gift Show with twenty handmade prototypes. Toobers & Zots were original, colorful, creative, and different. Before long, orders flew in, and the toy became a major national hit. Today, Hands On Toys continues its award-winning tradition with four lines of Toobers & Zots— Special, Classic, Magnetic, and Stick-On—plus craft-specific kits to foster more creativity.

ARTS AND CRAFTS

TERRIFIC TOOLS FOR THE ARTIST-TO-BE

From fingerpainting to Play-Doh, crayons to Colorforms, children's experiences with art help them expand their creativity, improve their ability to relate to the world, and appreciate the aesthetics of life. It doesn't matter what the specific art or craft is, as long as your child is enthusiastic about it. Let them try a variety of media, including chalk, clay, paper, paint, glue, yarn—you name it. Keep a creative box handy with a variety of magazines, cards, and paper for children to do collages with simple paste and construction paper. Brown butcher paper, newsprint, and non-stick white shelf paper are all excellent to have in abundance. Good manufacturers of art supplies are

Avalon, Binney & Smith, Colorforms, Dixon Ticonderoga, Doodletop, Fisher-Price, Kenner, Ohio Art, and Reeves International. In addition, craft kits by such companies as Alex, Creativity for Kids, and Educational Games provide children with excellent hands-on experiences and a lot of satisfaction.

With the opportunity to try out different art forms, children better understand colors and have a greater appreciation for their environment. They gain self-confidence and also learn to express emotions constructively. Remember to post their artwork on the wall or refrigerator to provide extra support and nurture their self-esteem. Children really enjoy expressing themselves, so parents should try to take time out and enjoy the experience with them. Many wonderful opportunities for creativity lie ahead for your child with the great products included here.

One way to encourage children to express their feelings is to suggest they draw, paint, or create a collage detailing a recent experience. Once they are finished, talk about what they have done. By providing this outlet, you'll be helping your child improve communication skills and gain another perspective on an experience.

With the variety of arts and crafts materials available, the opportunities for creativity are limitless. Fold an origami flower. Design a paper-doll world. Shape clay into creepy creatures. Weave yarn into colorful jewelry. Create costumes from felt. Accessorize an outfit with beads and string. Any idea your child may have can be realized by the wealth of great products available.

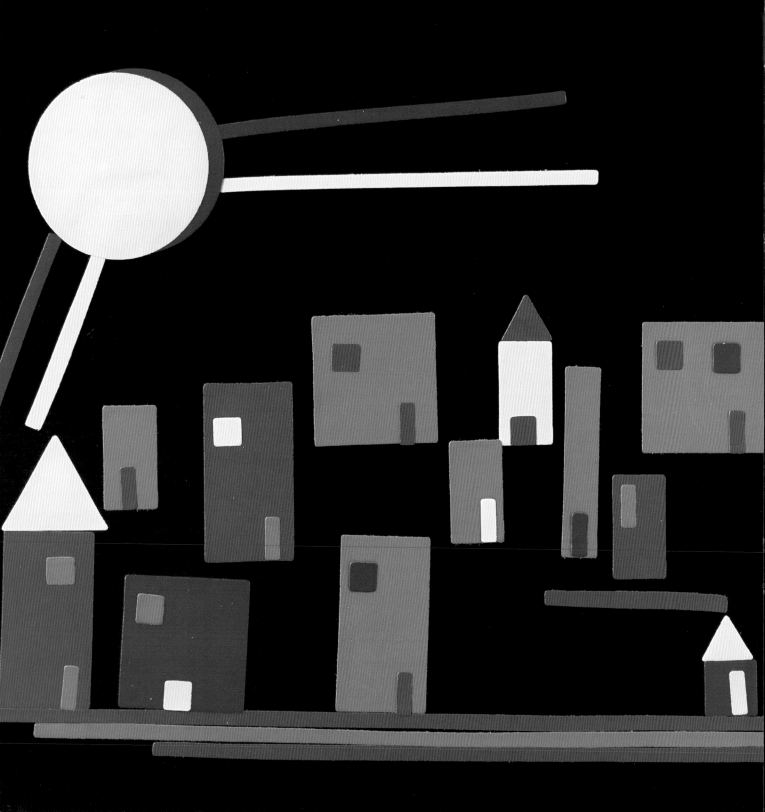

COLORFORMS

FUN THAT'S ANYTHING BUT FLAT

3–6 years

In 1951 two art students, Harry and Patricia Kislevitz, made the serendipitous discovery that vinyl sticks to semigloss paint. From this discovery, Colorforms were born.

The original set features basic, geometric shapes in bright, primary colors and a permanent, stick-on/take-off surface, all made from a clean, washable material. Colorforms can easily be attached to glossy surfaces and other Colorforms by applying slight pressure over the entire form. These simple but versatile shapes can be used together in endless, fascinating combinations, from a single figure to a whole series of designs. By using this toy, children learn basic shapes and colors, hone their perception of spatial relationships, improve manual dexterity, and express themselves artistically.

Colorforms has developed stick-ons with such popular licensed characters as Barbie and Mickey Mouse. The gifty black box and wide variety of shapes and colors make it a delight to use.

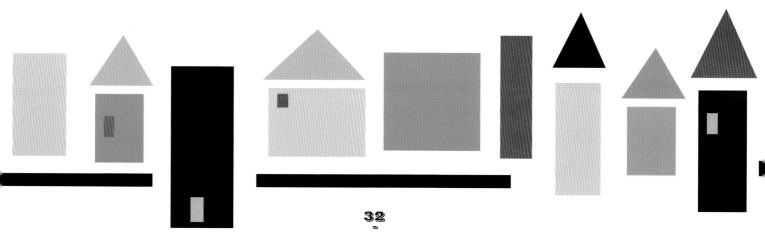

CRAYOLA CRAYONS

BRINGING OUT THE ARTIST IN ALL OF US

3–9 years

The Crayola crayon, made of simple paraffin wax and color pigments, has become a symbol of creativity throughout the world. The crayon is an inexpensive and delightfully simple way to encourage the artistic skills of any child. Binney & Smith, the manufacturer, makes the crayon in three sizes: Regular, Jumbo, and So Big. Your child can design a birthday card for Grandpa, a holiday greeting for his teacher, or a picture for his room.

The name Crayola was coined by joining the French word *craie* which means "chalk," with *ola*, from oleaginous or oily. Crayola crayons are made in ninety-six different colors, but their labels are made in only eighteen. Violet and blue-violet, for example, have the same color label. In the history of Crayola crayons, only two crayon colors—peach and midnight blue—have ever had their names changed. The color *flesh* became *peach* in 1962 as a result of the civil rights movement; while in 1958, *Prussian blue* was changed to *midnight blue* in response to teachers believing that children would no longer relate to Prussian history.

In 1864 Joseph W. Binney founded a company that made paint for barns and, later, for tires. The company continued to expand, experimenting with new chemical compounds to create new products. In 1885 Binney's son and nephew formed a partnership called Binney & Smith. At that time they diversified to produce shoe polish and printer's inks. In 1900 they purchased a mill and began producing pencils. This product introduced them to the educational market, and they began to see the opportunity to expand into the children's art field. First they developed chalk, and then crayons. In 1903 they developed nontoxic pigments and launched a new brand of crayons. A box with eight different colors retailed for about five cents that year.

ETCH-A-SKETCH

FOR ENDLESS HOURS OF ETCHING FUN

4 years and up

In its thirty-ninth year of production, Etch-A-Sketch has been called the "world's first laptop." Easy to use, this product allows both children and adults to make unique art creations that are easily erased. Using the knobs to control the movement of the lines, children can doodle, design, and draw and never make a permanent mistake. Its clean design and versatility make Etch-A-Sketch a great travel product. Over one hundred million children in sixty-seven countries have been drawn to the irresistible white knobs for endless hours of etching fun.

FAO SCHWARZ, 1962

Etch-A Sketch has changed little in the years since its introduction in 1960. It is still manufactured in Bryan, Ohio, and still comes in the classic red case, but its original brass knobs have been replaced with white plastic. Etch-A-Sketch is one of a fine line of arts-and-crafts products manufactured by Ohio Arts.

PARENTS: LET'S PLAY!

1. Determine your child's favorite activites and their skill level.
2. When you join in, let your child be in control and determine the direction of the play.
3. Remember, there isn't only one way to play with a toy—be imaginative.
4. Don't always use playtime to test or stretch your child's skills. The spontaneity of play is what makes it fun.

PLAY-DOH CASE OF COLOR

PERFECT CLAY FOR THE HANDS OF YOUNG SCULPTORS

3–8 years

Easy to use, Play-Doh can be squeezed, pulled, and molded into countless shapes—pizza pies, sand castles, you name it! The Case of Color ten-pack includes all the colors of the rainbow, plus black and brown. New products include Play-Doh soap—a moldable soap that kids can shape and lather—and Play-Doh Wacky Scents—with wild scents such as Explorange and Rose Garden—that will make it even harder to convince kids not to put the nontoxic Doh into their mouths.

Play-Doh was created in 1955 by teacher Joseph McVicer. His father owned Rainbow Crafts, a Cincinnati company that produced soap and cleaning solutions. McVicer was inspired by his sister-in-law's complaint that young students needed an alternative to modeling clay. The old-fashioned stuff was too hard and stiff for small hands to manipulate, and it dried out quickly. He came up with a modeling compound that was softer and more pliable and called it Play-Doh. In 1957 the wife of a Washington, D.C. department store buyer saw the grayish-white Play-Doh demonstrated at an educator's convention and sold the idea to her husband. Rainbow Crafts soon expanded the product by three colors—red, blue, and yellow.

In the fifties, the craft sets were licensed under Ding Dong School, a popular kindergarten TV show hosted by teacher Miss Frances. The Play-Doh Pete image, which appears as a packaging logo, was created, and the two-ounce minicans were introduced. In 1970 the five hundred millionth can of Play-Doh compound was sold. Since then, Play-Doh has expanded into playsets that include food-inspired sets (Pizza Party, Spaghetti, and Ice Cream); licensed sets (Barney, Mr. Potato Head, and Teletubbies); and just plain wacky sets (Fun Factory and Fuzzy Pumper Barber and Beauty Shop).

38

SPIROGRAPH

A CHILD'S SPIN ON GRAPHIC DESIGN

5–10 years

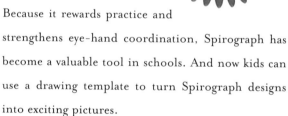

Spirograph's visual creativity and ease of use expands the range of art experiences for children. With its wild colors and patterns, Spirograph is appropriate for all ages and abilities.

Using a simple set of gear-form templates and a set of colored pens, anyone can make hundreds of geometric shapes and create a variety of effects. Because it rewards practice and strengthens eye-hand coordination, Spirograph has become a valuable tool in schools. And now kids can use a drawing template to turn Spirograph designs into exciting pictures.

The basic set includes seven gears, a gear template, a drawing template, a pen, and an idea book.

The Spirograph was created by Englishman Dennis Fischer, whose goal was to create a toy in which different patterns were guaranteed. Introduced in 1965 at the Nuremburg International Toy Fair, the Spirograph was spotted by Kenner, which assumed the American rights. Kenner is now owned by Hasbro. Since its introduction in the mid-sixties, more than thirty million Spirographs have been sold.

MAGNETIC DRAWING BOARD

AN EASY EASEL

3–7 years

This is an innovative drawing toy with many variations, including a Face Doodler, a Learning Bus, and Travel Magna Doodle. With its fine-line, magnetic drawing pen and six shape stampers, children can easily stamp, draw, and erase like magic and then start again. The Magna Doodle gives children confidence, because they are able to create recognizable images with ease. The stamps and eraser can also be used to teach simple addition and subtraction.

Magna Doodle Face Doodler easily makes a lot of different funny faces and helps children distinguish different facial features. It is shaped like an artist's palette and comes complete with five magnetic stampers and a magnetic brush. The parts are stored by locking them into the palette. It is great for trips.

Magna Doodle was created in 1974 at Pilot Pen Corporation of Japan by four engineers who were searching for a dustless chalkboard. What they found would eventually become one of the world's most popular drawing toys. Since then, Magna Doodle has had a variety of uses, including diagramming football plays and helping people in hospitals who cannot communicate. Now distributed by Fisher-Price, Magna Doodle has been purchased by more than forty million people.

Good Travel Toys

1. Activity books
2. Art pad and pencils
3. Books
4. Colorforms play sets
5. Etch-A-Sketch
6. Hand-held games
7. Hand-held puzzles
8. Paper dolls
9. Puppets
10. Cassette tapes

DOLLS, STUFFED ANIMALS,

GENE DOLL

Dolls, in all of their forms, provide a timeless way for children to relate to the world. Holding their little playmates offers children a positive, nurturing, and enjoyable experience, stimulates them to express language, and increases their self-expression. These figures can be a source of comfort to children when they are feeling upset and can help them work through a range of feelings, developmental stages, and social experiences. They also function as "transitional objects"—objects that can help a child cope with and moderate feelings associated with fear of separation or emotional upsets.

Young children make the leap from simply manipulating the doll or teddy to engaging it in social activities. Parents can encourage this transition by showing their children how to relate to the doll and how to care for it in a gentle way. When you share your affection with your child and her doll or teddy bear, you show her how to express love and experience the good feelings associated with it. And your child can transfer her feelings from her toy to a new sibling, pet kitten, or puppy. This can be very helpful when a new baby arrives, because a big brother or sister can better handle the adjustment. Caring for a doll or teddy bear while Mommy and Daddy care for the new baby helps your older child feel included and important.

These dolls, action figures, and stuffed animals often become companions for discovery. A young girl may take her bear when she explores the imaginary dark cave that holds monsters and a treasure; a boy's action figure may be the great sea captain's first mate in a battle against pirates. The possibilities are endless. But the doll may also be a partner in calmer pleasures. Your daughter may serve tea and cookies to her bear and to her playmates—some imaginary, some real. Your son

AND ACTION FIGURES
COMPANIONS TO DISCOVERY AND FRIENDS FOR LIFE

may take his to a make-believe ball game.

Playing with action figures makes children feel powerful and helps them develop a stronger sense of themselves and their capabilities. For example, by playing with a figure such as Superman or Wonder Woman, a child will be identifying with doing good deeds, saving lives, and being a hero or heroine. The personality and behavior of the character on which the action figure is based should therefore be carefully considered before purchasing.

The variety of plush toys, dolls, and action figures is endless. The range of dolls includes baby dolls, such as those by Corolle, soft dolls like Raggedy Ann and Andy, beautiful colectibles of Madame Alexander (one of the great pioneers in the doll field), and stylish Gene Dolls designed by Mel Odom (in honor of Gene Marshall, a moviestar from 1941 to 1962). Gund makes plush, huggable versions of hun-

GUND'S SNUFFLES

dreds of animals, including its wildly popular Snuffles bear. And there are action figures based on characters in movies (*Star Wars*, *Godzilla*), television shows (*Power Rangers*, *Teenage Mutant Ninja Turtles*), and comic books (*X-Men*, *Spawn*). Also, plenty of books serve as inspiration. When you read children stories featuring their favorite characters—such as Curious George,

STAR WARS STORM TROOPER

Arthur, or Madeline—the storybooks can stimulate children to dramatize the story with their figures and then to develop more elaborate scenarios.

Your children may hold certain dolls close to their hearts. Perhaps your daughter plays with a doll given to you by your mother (or grandmother). In that case, she is very lucky. Her doll not only anchors her to the family; it also makes her feel important. It is no small thing to be trusted with something old and valuable.

STEIFF TEDDY BEAR

A FRIEND INDEED

3–12 years

A teddy bear provides comfort and warmth to a child (and to many adults). Your gift of a teddy is precious and important, because the bear is often the treasured recipient of a child's affection and secrets. Treating a bear in a personal way, like naming it or planning its birthday party, stimulates communication skills and may lead to a discussion about manners, social graces, and appropriate party behavior. Being able to give the bear affection is another way that the bear can help a child gain self-confidence.

The bears made by the Steiff Company are very special, as is the company's story. The Steiff story began in Giengen, Germany, where Margarete Steiff was born in 1847. Although confined to a wheelchair because of polio, Margarete attended school like any other child and learned to sew. In 1879 she noticed a pattern in a magazine for a toy elephant and made a few to give as gifts. She went on to sew a bear, a poodle, and a donkey.

Margarete's stuffed animals proved so popular that she was able to turn her hobby into a business. Margarete's nephew Richard helped his aunt design and produce the company's stuffed toys. In 1902 Richard designed a series of jointed animals, including a monkey and a bear based on drawings he had made at the Stuttgart Zoo. On the last day of the 1903 Leipzig Fair, Hermann Berg, a buyer from New York, visited the Steiff booth and immediately fell in love. The following year, Richard Steiff went to America to visit the World's Fair in St. Louis. Much to Margarete's delight, Richard came home with substantial orders. Not only was the Steiff bear a hit, it had won gold medals and the prestigious Grand Prix Award. Since then, the Steiff bears, with their jointed arms and legs and trademark metal button in their left ear, have been treasured the world over.

ACTIVITY DOLL

A CHILD'S GUIDE TO GETTING DRESSED

6 months–3 years

This fourteen-inch-long activity clown has many wonderful qualities and features. It's soft, huggable, and washable and has a rattle, a zipper, a Velcro fastener, buttons and a buttonhole, and laced shoes.

All these features are helpful to a child learning to dress himself, an important part of becoming independent. Your child will practice fine motor skills by manipulating the buttons, ties, zippers, and snaps on the clown. This is a wonderful toy to have both at home and at day care, when your son or daughter is toilet training and is learning to dress and undress.

This irresistible clown is made in Sweden by BRIO, the world's largest manufacturer of wooden toys. In 1884 three young brothers began making high-quality wooden toys in Osby, Sweden. The BRIO Corporation got its name from those *Brothers Ivarsson* of *Osby*. Peter Reynolds began distributing BRIO toys in the United States in 1977. BRIO makes good toys that are safe and durable and encourage open-ended play.

Top Children's Videos

1. *Shari Lewis* (Columbia Tri-Star)
2. *Muppets, School House Rock, Winnie the Pooh* (Disney Home Video)
3. *Dr. Seuss* (Fox Home Entertainment)
4. *Baby Sitter's Club* (Kidvision)
5. *Barney* (Lyrick Studio)
6. *Music for Little People*
7. *Geo Kids* (National Geographic)
8. *PBS Nature Series* (Nature Video Library)
9. *Teletubbies* (PBS Home Video/Warner)
10. *Blue's Clues, Rugrats* (Paramount Home Video)
11. *Rock 'n' Learn*
12. *Berenstain Bears, Madeline, Richard Scarry, Sesame Street* (Sony Wonder)

CABBAGE PATCH KIDS

A DOLL AS UNIQUE AS YOUR CHILD

3—12 years

The doll that sprouted from a cabbage patch in 1983 to take the world by storm is still going strong as one of the most popular toys ever. Over the past sixteen years, more than ninety million Cabbage Patch Kids have been "adopted" into homes all over the world. Children have a special relationship with their Cabbage Patch Kids. Adopting a Cabbage Patch Kid allows girls and boys the opportunity to form a nurturing and enduring relationship with their very own 'Kid. Each one of the soft and huggable Cabbage Patch Kids is one-of-a-kind, with unique facial expressions; hair, body and eye color; hairstyle; name; and birth date. The Cabbage Patch Kids are soft, cuddly, and can be cleaned with a soft cloth. Since all of the clothes are washable, the 'Kid can get into all sorts of adventures with your child.

When Georgia artist Xavier Roberts created the original soft sculpture, he knew he had something special. When he conceptualized the idea of "adoption" papers and began the original Appalachian Dolls Company (now owned by Mattel), Cabbage Patch Dolls became an instant hit. The adoption papers include the date of birth, the 'Kid's name, a family history, footprints and thumbprints, and one unique characteristic. A reply card ensures that a birthday card will be sent annually to each 'Kid.

· TOYS I REMEMBER ·

When I was eighteen months old, my father bought me a toy chimpanzee. He was named Jubilee after the first chimpanzee to be born at the London Zoo—during the Jubilee Year of the King and Queen. My parents' friends predicted the "creature" (some 2 ½ feet tall) would give me nightmares. In fact, Jubilee was my favorite toy and accompanied me everywhere during my first ten years. I still have him today—hairless from love!

—JANE GOODALL, naturalist

RAGGEDY ANN AND ANDY

DOLLS TO LOVE FOR YEARS AND YEARS

3–8 years

Raggedy Ann has been America's favorite soft doll for more than eighty years—the longest-running character license in the toy industry. Cartoonist and illustrator Johnny Gruelle worked with his daughter, Marcella, to create Raggedy Ann out of an old rag doll found in an attic. Realizing the character's potential, Gruelle secured a patent and trademark for his design in 1915. Meanwhile, Marcella contracted smallpox and died. In her memory, Gruelle wrote and illustrated the *Raggedy Ann Stories.* In 1918 the Volland Company followed up on the success of the book with the first Raggedy Ann doll. Ann's spirited brother, Andy, arrived two short years later.

Traditional Raggedy Ann and Andy dolls—both in red, white, and blue outfits, with soft yarn hair and the characteristic tiny red heart—are sure to please both children and collectors of all ages. Again, playing with a doll that is soft and cuddly is a wonderful opportunity for the child to express emotion. And any doll whose heart plainly states her affection ("I Love You" is printed in the heart of every doll) should easily elicit emotion from your child. Reading the stories while holding the dolls can be a valuable experience for any child.

RAGGEDY FACTS

1. *There is an annual festival celebrating Raggedy Ann in Arcola, Illinois, the birthplace of her creator.*

2. *The first Raggedy Anns produced by Volland contained a die-cut cardboard heart that could be felt in the doll's chest.*

3. *In 1997 the United States Postal Service issued a Raggedy Ann stamp, one of fifteen classic American doll stamps.*

BARBIE BITS

- On average, all girls between three and ten own at least one Barbie doll. The dolls are sold in 140 countries.

- Two Barbie dolls are sold every second somewhere in the world.

- Since 1955, more than 125 million yards of fabric have gone into making Barbie's clothing. More than one billion pairs of shoes have been manufactured.

- Barbie has been modified over the years to reflect different ethnic and cultural differences.

- Boyfriend Ken was introduced in 1961, friend Midge in 1963, and sister Skipper in 1964.

BARBIE

A GIRL'S PERFECT PLAYMATE

5—12 years

With companions Ken, Skipper, and Midge, Barbie stimulates role-playing and fantasy play. By employing the wide range of amazing accessories—her house, car, shoes, plus those for one of the selected careers—little girls transform a Barbie doll into a positive playmate. When girls play with Barbie, they communicate, share secrets, try out different roles, and experience a world of fun and fantasy. While some have criticized Barbie for being an unrealistic physical ideal, she allows girls the chance to play out their own dreams. Therefore, using Barbie as a role model helps girls better understand themselves.

The idea for the Barbie doll was born in a mom's observations. Ruth Handler, one of the founders of Mattel, watched her daughter, Barbara, play with paper dolls. She realized that pretend play was an important part of growing up. When she created the Barbie doll, she was also creating a unique innovation in dolls. At the time of the Barbie doll's introduction in 1955, the only other dolls available were babies and toddlers. Barbie made an impact almost from the start.

Since then, Barbie has led the way in design, fashion, and fantasy. She started off as a teenage fashion model. Through the years, Barbie has changed her focus but has never lost her style. She has reflected the times and variances of fashion. While she has many different looks—from rock star to executive—she can always be transformed by a little girl's imagination.

Today Barbie has expanded her role again, this time into fashion design. Barbie Fashion Designer CD-ROM, a unique software, offers little girls the chance to create their own play clothing. They can print patterns, use color and decorations, and assemble their designs. This software also helps girls experience new technology.

Barbie offers girls the fun of playing with many accessories, dreaming, and enjoying fantasy play.

G.I. JOE

FOR THE FEARLESS ADVENTURER IN ANY CHILD

5–12 years

G.I. Joe's first battle was to overcome the 1960's notion that boys did not want to play with dolls. His success proved to the world that boys were interested in toys that inspired their imaginations and empowered them, thus spawning today's billion-dollar action-figure category. By playacting, children can transfer themselves into another era and pique their interest in military history. G.I. Joe also fosters social play by giving children something to talk about and playact together.

Originally there were four G.I. Joe action figures, one each for the Army, Navy, Air Force, and Marines. The goal was to teach children the strong basic values that G.I. Joe represents: honor, courage, respect, service, and, of course, good clean fun. Five short years after its debut, G.I. Joe was the number-one-selling toy among boys five to twelve years old.

Originally 11½ inches tall with twenty-one moving parts, the doll was named Joe after the movie *The Story of G.I. Joe*, starring Robert Mitchum. Whether rafting through raging rapids (in bathtubs), planning battle strategy (in tree houses), or driving his rugged vehicles (through muddy backyards), the world's first action figure is always suitably attired. Accessories include uniforms for each branch of the service, weapons from hand grenades to bazookas, and military gear from helmets to canteens.

THE MANY FACES OF G.I. JOE

- *In 1974, during the kung fu craze, some G.I. Joe figures acquired a kung fu handgrip.*
- *In 1975 G.I. Joe introduced bionic warrior Atomic Man. More than one million figures were sold.*
- *In 1986, professional wrestler Sgt. Slaughter became the first real-life person to become a member of G.I. Joe Corps.*
- *By 1993 over 250 million G.I. Joe figures and 115 million vehicles had been sold.*
- *In 1997 the first G.I. Joe female fighting figure, a U.S. Army helicopter pilot, was introduced.*

WINNIE THE POOH

A KIND, COMFORTING COMPANION

1–7 years

A.A. Milne was inspired by his wife, Daphne, and his young son, Christopher Robin, to write the poems and stories of Winnie the Pooh. These whimsical stories gave birth to a plush doll, whose delightful persona has made him a favorite of children around the world.

The literary journey began in 1924, when Christopher Robin was introduced to a bear at the London Zoological Gardens. This and subsequent meetings inspired a series of books based on the love between a boy and his bear (as well as the adventures of the bear's many companions: Piglet, Eeyore, Owl, Rabbit, Kanga and Roo, and, of course, Tigger).

Because his story is so well known, Winnie the Pooh can come alive to your child with his own personality and speech. And, as your child begins to interact with others, this lovable bear can serve as something to talk about or to playact together, helping initiate your child's early attempts at social interaction. And the bear's nonsensical sense encourages you to want to read aloud with your child to make the most of Pooh's experience.

Winnie the Pooh plush dolls come in numerous sizes and are produced by a variety of companies, including Mattel and Applause. There is even an interactive Pooh CD-ROM that lets children enjoy computer games and activities with their cuddly friend.

TEDDY'S BEAR

President Theodore Roosevelt was largely responsible for the success of the stuffed bear in the United States. Known as "Teddy" to his friends, Roosevelt was an avid hunter. In 1902, on a four-day hunting trip in Mississippi, the president refused to shoot a young bear that had been captured for him. The Washington Post *cartoonist Clifford Berryman captured the incident in a now-famous cartoon, and the lucky bear became known as "Teddy's bear." It wasn't long before a stuffed version of the Teddy bear captured the hearts of Americans and the rest of the world.*

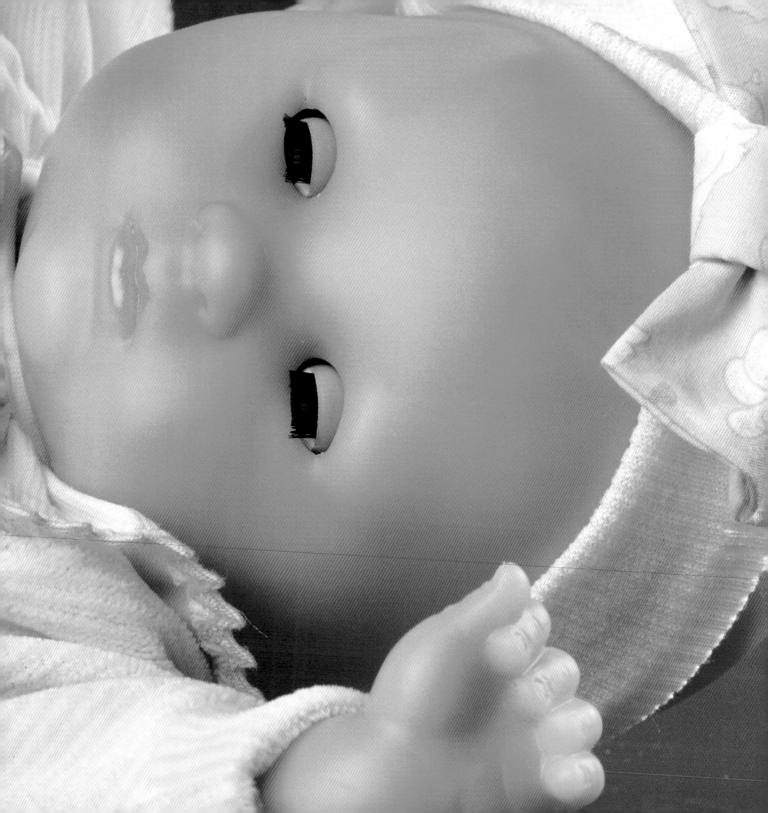

BABY DOLL

A BABY FOR YOUR BABY TO BABY

3–9 years

Corolle dolls are set apart from all others by their sweet, expressive faces, quality materials and construction, and creative fashions. They are designed to appeal to a child's heart and inspire endless hours of fulfilling fantasy play. The soft baby doll is fourteen inches tall, with vanilla-scented vinyl limbs and head.

This doll is easy for your little one to carry, and your child will benefit from the nurturing experience it provides. The dolls are delightful for pretend play, which can include dressing, feeding, talking, and singing the baby doll to sleep. The dolls also have many accessories, such as suitcases and other travel items.

The dolls Corolle creates encourage the child to explore different roles through caring and sharing with a new friend. Dressed in current French clothing, the dolls are designed to resemble real babies: the eyes are proportional to the human face; the hair imitates real children's hair; and the doll's weight is proportional to the weight of a child. Sized to fit in a child's arms, these dolls are machine-washable, durable, and meant to last a lifetime.

Corolle means "the heart of a flower." The original company, Clodrey, was founded by Jacques Refabert in 1952. In 1996 the company developed many new designs with its new president, Catherine Petot, whose background is in children's fashion.

GAMES

CHALLENGE AND COMPETITION FOR ALL AGES

As children grow they benefit from playing games, which help them to develop social relationships, play fairly, share, take turns, and cope with wins and losses. Games can provide an early lesson in the value of good sportsmanship and how to compete positively.

The old axiom, "It's not whether you win or lose but how you play the game," is especially important with children. Many are able to learn so much so fast that parents sometimes forget that their little dynamo might not really understand what a game is, much less how a particular game works. Make sure to teach your children the rules of a game. Read the rules out loud and make sure they are clear to everyone playing. The more children understand, the more satisfied (and rightfully proud) they will be when they win. Rules provide the structure and background for fun.

When considering a game for your child, you need to determine your child's interests, personality, and skill level—otherwise you won't really know what your child can handle. In games for very young children, winning should depend more on chance than on skill. That way, a four-year-old novice can sometimes experience the satisfaction of beating a parent or older sibling. Until children become really adept at a particular game and have solid social instincts, keep a close watch on them. Your presence can prevent many childish catastrophes, such as cheating, and turn seemingly insurmountable problems into solutions. If your levelheadedness saves the day, children may copy this behavior and employ it themselves.

Learning and literacy games challenge your child to match or identify pictures, letters, and words by making associations. The questions these games pose are the same types of question-and-answer thinking we go through in daily life. If you observe that your child is uncertain about how to proceed, ask, "What do you think comes next?" If your child is still uncertain, encourage her to try one way or another. However, by leaving the final answer up to your child, you help her practice valuable thinking skills.

Board games also offer an opportunity for all ages to play together. Inviting other children over to play games is a great way for your child to develop social relationships. Children begin to learn from each other the rules that make playing together work—that it's better to share, wait your turn, and be nice to others so they'll be nice back. Family game night is also a great way to spend quality family time.

Beyond sociability and encouraging problem-solving, many games enhance specific skills. For example, learning colors, shapes, and numbers can start with the classic game Candyland. Children can increase their vocabulary and learn to spell by playing games such as Scrabble or Boggle. Children learn about adult responsibilities and roles when they play games like Monopoly, Careers, or Life. Games by Aristoplay can even help children with schoolwork. Other family favorites are Go to the Head of the Class, Easy Money, Operation, Battleship, and Yahtzee.

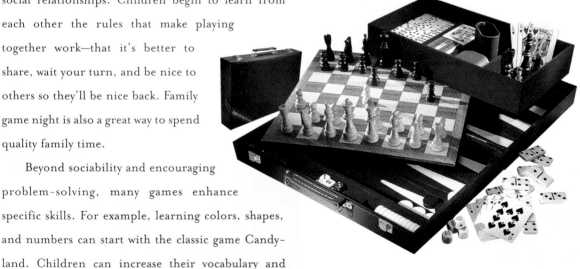

GLOPPY

MOLASSES SWAMP

STUCK IN MOLASSES SWAMP
STAY HERE UNTIL
A ■ CARD IS DRAWN

LOLLIPOP WOO

GRAMMA NUTT

CANDYLAND

A CHILD'S FIRST TASTE OF VICTORY

3–6 years

Candyland is a good first game for a child for a variety of reasons—it teaches socialization and how to learn rules, follow directions, and identify colors. Constructed for two to four players from ages three and up, it is a fun game for the whole family to play. Once a child can recognize basic colors, that child has an equal opportunity to win the game.

"The Legend of the Lost Candy Castle," a once-upon-a-time story about all of the Candyland characters, is printed on the inside of the box and can be read out loud to set the tone before the game begins. The overall structure of the game is as follows: Players, represented by plastic ginger-bread men in different colors, draw cards that advance them along the rainbow path through the different areas of Candyland, including Peppermint Stick Forest, Gingerbread Plum Tree, and Gumdrop Mountain. The object is to be the first player to reach the last purple space or to move beyond the last purple space to reach King Kandy's missing candy castle. But you must be aware of the barriers along the way, like being trapped in a wreath of gooey gumdrops, lost in the lollipop woods, or stuck in the molasses swamp. With easy-to-store pieces, the game board is colorful and has lots of yummy candy references.

And where did this sweet game originate? Eleanor Abbott of San Diego, California, while recuperating from polio in 1940, occupied herself by devising games and activities for children with the same affliction. One of her inventions was Candyland. Her friends liked the game and submitted it to Milton Bradley. It was accepted and introduced to the public in 1949. Candyland has remained a big hit ever since.

PICTIONARY

COMBINING CREATIVITY WITH COMPETITION

12 years and up

You don't need to be Rembrandt to win at Pictionary—you just need rudimentary drawing skills, a good vocabulary, and a strong imagination. The goal of the game, besides having a good time, is to sketch your way around the game board with your teammate, taking turns guessing what the other is trying to draw. Whichever team reaches the end first wins.

This game is ideal for older children and adults, because the rules are fairly complex and you need a good grasp of spelling and vocabulary to succeed. Each team of two or more players chooses a picturist (the person who sketches). The sketches should be simple—stick figures and squiggly lines will do fine. The picturist takes a card and, without speaking, sketches the word or phrase corresponding to the square that the team's marker is on. (If it's an ALL PLAY, a picturist from each team sketches the same word at the same time.) The sand timer is turned over. Your team (all teams if it's an ALL PLAY) now has one minute to guess. If you guess correctly before the time is up, you roll the dice and move on. If not, you stay where you are.

Pictionary enhances word comprehension and creative thinking. Picturists can draw synonyms for their word (*mail* for *male* or *blew* for *blue*); break the word down into syllables; and draw anything related to the word, no matter how tenuous the link.

CHUTES AND LADDERS

LEARNING YOUR DOS AND DON'TS THE FUN WAY

4–7 years

Chutes and Ladders is a delightful game that is easy to play, even for children who can't read yet. Fun pictures help them understand the rewards of doing good deeds as they climb up the ladders—and the consequences of naughty ones as they slide down the chutes.

The object of the whirlwind Chutes and Ladders game is to be the first player to reach square number 100. Represented by a cardboard-kid pawn, you flick the spinner and move your pawn to the square with the number shown by the spinner. If you land on a ladder, you move up to the square at the end of the ladder. If you land on a chute, you slide back to the bottom.

Chutes and Ladders is actually based upon an old game called Snakes and Ladders that European settlers brought with them to America. It was first developed and sold to game giant Milton Bradley in 1943.

SCRABBLE

THE WORD-BUILDING GAME EVEN ADULTS CAN PLAY

6 years and up

What has one hundred tiles, 225 squares, a multicolored board, and millions of fans of all ages and backgrounds? The answer is Scrabble. This great classic game helps children learn new words and practice spelling and language skills. Played with two to four players, it is a game that the whole family can enjoy together.

During the Great Depression of the 1930s, Alfred M. Butts, an out-of-work architect from Poughkeepsie, New York, decided to invent a board game called Criss Cross Words which depended both on luck and skill. After calculating the frequency of the twenty-six letters of the alphabet by looking at the front page of the *New York Times*, Butts created a game that combined the features of anagrams with crossword puzzles. Butts drew his first Criss Cross Words game with his architectural drafting equipment, reproducing it by blueprinting it and pasting it on a folding checkerboard. The hand-lettered tiles were then glued to quarter-inch pieces of balsa and cut to match the squares on the board.

Although the game has changed in some ways since 1948, Butts's analysis of letter frequency, his original tile distribution, his fifteen-by-fifteen-inch symmetrical square board pattern, and his rule specifying seven available tiles per turn have remained unchanged.

Scrabble is one of the leading board games in America, and it is the country's most popular word game. Competitive Scrabble is very popular, much like chess and bridge. Every other year the National Scrabble Championship is held in a major United States city. The World Scrabble Championship—which attracts players from thirty-one countries—is alternately hosted by the United States and England.

SORRY!

FOR HOURS OF FAMILY FUN

6 years and up

Sorry! has been enhancing kids' fun since 1934. The object of the game is to be the first player to get all four of the pawns in your starting color into that color's home. Sorry! has a game board, a deck of cards, and four pawns in each of the four colors. Players choose four pawns of the same color, put all four on the start space, shuffle the deck, place it facedown, and pick the player to go first. If it's your turn first, and you do not draw a card that lets you start a pawn, you forfeit your turn. You must bring your pawns into home by exact count. Once a pawn reaches home, you don't move that piece again for the rest of the game. The winner is the first player to get all four pawns home. Sorry! can also be played as a team game. Red is always yellow's partner; green is always blue's partner. There are special variations of Sorry! for adults, so everyone can play and enjoy the game. The newest edition on CD-ROM, produced by Hasbro Interactive, has pawns that slip and slide around the board, taunting and teasing the other pawns along the way. Any way you play it, Sorry! is an easy and fun way to bring friends and family together.

FAO SCHWARZ CATALOG, 1954

Monopoly Moments

©1936 Hasbro, Inc.

- More than two hundred million games have been sold worldwide.

- More than five billion little green houses have been "built" since 1935.

- In 1978, Neiman Marcus offered an all-chocolate Monopoly set for $600.

- The longest Monopoly game in history lasted seventy straight days.

- The longest Monopoly game in a bathtub lasted ninety-nine hours.

MONOPOLY

A GAME FOR YOUNG ENTREPRENEURS

5 years and up

The original Monopoly, which debuted in 1935, almost did not make it to market. In the height of the depression, Charles B. Darrow of Germantown, Pennsylvania, showed a game he called Monopoly to the executives at Parker Brothers. Parker Brothers initially rejected the game, citing "fifty-two design errors." But Mr. Darrow did not give up. Like many other Americans, he was unemployed at the time, and his dream that the game could bring him fame and fortune inspired him to produce it on his own.

With help from a friend who was a printer, Mr. Darrow sold five thousand handmade sets of the game to a Philadelphia department store. People loved it! But as demand grew, he couldn't keep up with all the orders and went to talk to Parker Brothers again. This time he met with success. During its first year on the market, Monopoly was the best-selling game in America. And over its sixty-five-year history, an estimated five hundred million people have played the game. It is the best-selling board game in the world, licensed or sold in eighty countries and produced in twenty-six languages. The Monopoly game is so much a part of today's popular culture that many of its graphic elements are trademarked. The tokens, railroads, community chest, chance card, title deed designs, Boardwalk, and game-board corners are legally protected.

Now younger family members can join in the Monopoly game experience with Monopoly Jr., a version for ages five through eight. Come join the Pennybags gang for a fun-filled day at Boardwalk Amusements. Set up ticket booths at the amusements and collect fees from other players who land on them. When you set up booths on two amusements of the same color, you collect double. Draw a chance card and take a ride on the miniature railroad—or pay three dollars to visit the rest rooms. When someone finally runs out of money, the player with the most cash on hand wins. Young players practice addition, subtraction, and multiplication as they collect fees, double fees, and make change.

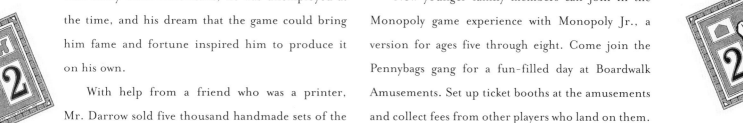

TRANSPORTATION TOYS

PLANES, TRAINS, AND AUTOMOBILES

The wonderful world of transportation toys reflects the dramatic history of ever-changing technology. In this wide range of products one can find the realistic, the fanciful, and the visionary—from horses to jet planes, sailboats to space capsules, emergency vehicles to trains to racing-car replicas. These toys can be constructed from the most basic wood or the sleekest metal.

Miniature racing cars replicate the latest models and styles of real cars. They have detailing right down to the trim and the sponsors' names. Collecting these vehicles appeals to a wide variety of enthusiasts, who know all about the actual vehicle's horsepower, drivers, and racing history.

Wooden toys combine imaginative opportunities with realistic play. A train is a perfect toy in the hands of the very small child, who thrills at his ability to move it around a track or to use it to haul dirt and sand from one place to another.

As children mature, they learn quickly about all the vehicles in their communities. Playing with toy trucks and creating the sounds of energy and motion provides hours of fun and role-playing to little drivers. Sailing boats in the backyard, in the bathtub, or in a large pond is a great treat. Young children are thrilled to make vehicles of all kinds move. This play may lead older children to the designing and construction of motors, radio-controlled cars, and train switches. They may fly a kite to experiment with wind power or learn about electricity through building their own train tracks. These toys have inspired generations of builders and inventors.

By introducing products like a dump truck or a racing car, you are giving your child new ways to express and expand her sense of the world's possibilities. And that's where inventions come from. Manipulating toys gives your child a sense of mastery, which builds self-confidence. Self-confidence makes for increased capacity and desire to learn.

Most of all, transportation toys help children

experience adult life in an exciting, accessible way. Don a cap, add a whistle, and it's "all aboard!" for a fun-filled adventure. Add books, so your little engineer can learn about the history of transportation and how moving things work and are made. Add tapes and other accessories, and the world of transportation grows even wider.

dance throughout the country and around the world. Many different companies make toys for the young enthusiast as well as the seasoned collector. The companies that make transportation toys include Mattel, Hasbro, Lionel, Learning Curve, and Galoob; companies such as Burago, Ertl, Hess, and Marx manufacture collector-quality cars.

Taking a trip in a real vehicle—a bus, a plane, a train, or a boat—reinforces and intensifies the play experience and makes it all the more meaningful. Travel is one of the most exciting experiences young children can have, and they learn so much from it.

Collecting is also a very popular hobby for both children and adults. There are collector clubs for Matchbox and Hot Wheels. Model-train enthusiasts and active toy-train collectors can be found in abun-

WOODEN FIGURE-8 TRAIN

TERRIFIC TRAINS FOR THE YOUNGEST ENGINEERS

2–5 years

BRIO's Wooden Figure-8 Train Set is a terrific, colorful, and practical starter set for young children. With its ease of design, this is a toy that really *helps* children. They are able to put the track pieces together and create their own personal route. Children have great fun moving their trains around, and when two children combine their toys, playtime is more than first-rate fun. The children learn to work together, to communicate problem-solving ideas, and to think ahead while simultaneously enhancing eye-hand coordination and dexterity. The train layout will give your children many hours of play.

This high-quality Swedish product is crafted of durable beechwood and painted with primary colors. These nontoxic paints are absorbed into the wood, making it particularly long-lasting and protecting it against chipping, peeling, and cracking.

The starter set has an engine, two wagons, a switching track, a straight track, and a viaduct. The magnetic coupling allows a child to attach the wagons with ease. The curved track is grooved on both sides, so it's reversible, and the modular system allows new sections to be added easily. The wooden train can grow with the child by adding more tracks, one or two bridges, more trains, and other accessories.

You can "test-drive" your child's likely reaction to the train by watching the children who gather around the BRIO train layout at FAO Schwarz stores. Stand at the track and watch all those little engineering heads spinning. When this generation grows up, America is bound to have lots of new high-speed trains.

Founded in 1884, BRIO is the largest wooden-toy manufacturer in the world. Its toys are safe, durable, open-ended playthings that allow your child to be creative and play to the fullest imagination.

Tonka Tidbits

- In 1949 Mount Metalcraft made thirteen different Tonka vehicles. Between 1949 and 1951 the company branched out and also made dolls' beds.

- In 1959, when the company changed its name to Tonka Trucks, it sold forty-three models.

- Tonka has made miniature trucks for Allied Van Lines, Green Giant, and Starkist Tuna.

- In 1961 Tonka purchased a plastics company and started selling accessories for the cars and trucks.

- More than 230 million Tonka trucks have been manufactured to date.

- For the fiftieth anniversary of the Tonka dump truck, a replica was created of the classic truck with all-steel construction, real rubber tires, authentic styling, and special packaging.

DUMP TRUCK

A CHILD'S FIRST REAL TRUCK

3–7 years

When children play with the Tonka dump truck, they do more than imagine construction work. They can, on a simple level, actually perform some standard construction-site tasks, such as loading, dumping, and maneuvering to avoid careening into a construction hole. Play verging on reality doesn't get any better than this. The Tonka dump truck is large and ready to be filled with small stones or objects, driven around the construction site, and turned and dumped. And this toy encourages language development ("Where should we put this load of dirt?"); develops eye-hand coordination ("How are we going to shore up the side of this building?"); and increases a sense of spatial relations ("Is there room to go between those two cars?").

As language develops, toddlers vocalize while playing with the truck. Their playtime gets more and more sophisticated as they put objects into the truck and move the vehicle around. They might bring the vehicle to their train set, have the train bring in a load of cargo, transfer the cargo to the truck, drive it to the construction site, dump the cargo, reload, and drive the new load back to the train for transport to a shipyard or airfield. Visiting construction sites to see real trucks at work will encourage your toddler to copy what he sees.

The Tonka dump truck began as an idea in Mound, Minnesota. Lynn Baker, Avery Crounse, and Alvin Tesch, owners of a modest metal stamping business, launched their first toy truck in 1947. It was a commercial failure. Determined to learn from that experience, they asked boys what they wanted in a toy. Boys wanted sturdy, strong, and real trucks—just like the ones on the highway. The owners went back to their workshop and designed a steam shovel and crane, both made of steel and with working parts. They were stamped with the word *Tonka*, which means "great" in Dakota Sioux, the language of the Native American tribe indigenous to Minnesota. The relaunch was an obvious success!

HOT WHEELS

FUN AT ANY SPEED

5–12 years

In 1968 Mattel introduced Hot Wheels miniature cars with minimal-friction wheels. These cars ran on track and could move very fast with just the slightest push. From that moment, the races were on.

Mattel went on to create elaborate layouts for the track that children can shape into loops for cars to zip through. There is a dash-and-crash set that can handle five cars, each of which move independently for high-speed, nonstop action. What really makes these cars fly off the shelves is their speed.

Thirty years ago, the first in-house Hot Wheels design was created by Ira Gilford to reflect the flash and power of a custom hot rod. (This later became the flagship car for the thirtieth anniversary of Hot Wheels cars.) Since then, this product line has reflected the history of car design. Hot Wheels offers a line of cool, die-cast cars in a variety of themes at scales of $\frac{1}{64}$, $\frac{1}{24}$, $\frac{1}{18}$, and $\frac{1}{48}$. The ultimate in die-cast collectibles is the Hot Wheels Legends To Life series, with cars that feature movable parts, working lights, engine noises, and meticulous detailing. While small in scale, these cars enable a child to drive three hundred miles an hour in his imagination.

Hot Wheels also teams up with some of the best racers and manufacturers in the business to create signature cars. One series has removable bodies and craftsmanship to scale and is endorsed by a select group of race-car drivers including Kyle Petty, who drives the #44 Hot Wheels Pontiac Grand Prix. In 1999 Mattel teamed up with Ferrari, one of the world's most prestigious names in automobiles, to create intricate vintage and contemporary reproductions in a variety of scales.

The wave of the future is the Hot Wheels Custom Car Designer CD-ROM, which allows children to print out stickers to decorate their Hot Wheels cars and track. Mattel is a leader in die-cast vehicles, play sets, and track.

ELECTRIC TRAINS

A CHERISHED TRADITION STAYS ON TRACK

8 years and up

Lionel trains will provide hours of fun for any young engineer. The realistic detailing encourages children to create a layout to go with the train, hence developing confidence. Bringing books about trains into their experience adds to their enjoyment and knowledge.

One special set, the New York Central Flyer Freight Set, has many realistic features, including a die-cast steam loco-

FAO SCHWARZ CATALOG, 1929

motive that puffs smoke and blasts warning signals with its authentic-sounding steam whistle. This steam locomotive will go with your child wherever she wants it to go. It also pulls boxcars, a flatcar carrying two vintage cars, a trailer, an animated log dump car, and an illuminated caboose. In addition, the set has grade crossings and a forty-watt, power-control system.

Generations of children have enjoyed a toy that was originally designed as a window display. In 1900, Joshua Lionel Cowen founded the Lionel Manufacturing Company close to New York's City Hall. He produced the first Lionel Train, the Electric Express, as a display designed to attract more visitors to stores by making window-shopping exciting. When Robert Ingersoll, a toy-and-novelty retailer in Manhattan, put the train in his window, he lured people into his store. But his new customers did not want his merchandise—they wanted the train. Since these humble beginnings, Lionel Trains has grown to produce more than one million engines, cabooses, and other railroad cars a year.

Traditionally found circling the Christmas tree, these trains have become an engrossing, year-round pastime for numerous fans and collectors. Many enthusiasts make the pilgrimage to the company's visitor center in Chesterfield, Michigan, to view the eight-train, 560-square-foot layout, built by company volunteers.

Big Things, Small Packages

• The NB-Model A Van, first issued in 1982, is the most popular Matchbox to date. One variation, with the Kellogg's logo on the side, has sold more than three million.

• The Matchbox name originated from the packaging Jack Odell created to enable his daughter to bring an early model to school.

MATCHBOX CARS

A CHILD'S FIRST COLLECTIBLE

5–12 years

For more than forty years, Matchbox vehicles have provided kids with all the excitement and entertainment of real-driving adventures. Whether appealing to boys' fascination with building things and knocking them down or offering the finely crafted, die-cast collectibles made especially for the adult collector, Matchbox is invariably synonymous with tradition and value.

It all dates back to 1947, when former schoolmates Rodney Smith and Leslie Smith returned to England from World War II determined to start their own company. They combined their names and resources to start a metal-manufacturing firm, Lesney Products. To increase production, they began manufacturing and marketing a souvenir version of the British Royal State Coach to commemorate the coronation of Queen Elizabeth II in 1952. The toy coach was wildly successful, and Lesney Products soon became full-time producers of miniature, die-cast cars.

FAO SCHWARZ CATALOG, 1968

In 1954 Jack Odell, the third partner in the company, created the models for the first series of Matchbox cars, which featured a road roller, dump truck, cement mixer, and tractor. In the line, and on-line, today (check out www.Matchbox.com), there are trucks, fire trucks, police cars, ambulances, and special vehicles such as a '33 Ford, a '56 Ford pickup, and a '57 Chevy. There are small-scale replicas of excavating trucks, Peterbilt cement trucks, utility trucks—even trucks shaped like animals, for example, a rhinoceros and an alligator. For the high-tech youngster, Action System playsets and computer games with realistic 3-D environments have been introduced to much acclaim.

RADIO-CONTROLLED CARS

SAFE EXCITEMENT ON AND OFF ROAD

7–12 years

Radio-controlled cars and trucks add an extra wallop to fantasy play involving speed, dexterity, and skill. They can take corners like race cars and maneuver over boulders like real monster trucks. With controls in hand, children can take charge and feel powerful.

Prior to 1986, radio-controlled vehicles weren't available in toy stores. They were exclusive to hobby shops as two-hundred-dollar gas-powered kits. Adults and young adults would build their vehicles, tune them up, and race them with real gasoline—not exactly a kid's hobby.

Turbo Hopper was the first Tyco R/C vehicle and the first affordable, mass-produced R/C toy that simply required batteries and was ready to go. Turbo Hopper was not only ready to go, it was ready to go anywhere! Four big knobby tires with generous suspension allowed the vehicle to race on dirt, on blacktop, and over hills, and to bounce off curbs. Turbo Hopper became available in October 1986 and was a complete sellout by November. A new toy category was born.

Each year since, a new series of R/C vehicles has been launched by Tyco. Highlights include Typhoon (1989), which traveled on land as well as on water; Fast Traxx (1991), the fastest and best-selling R/C vehicle ever, featuring twin, independent motors to double the fun; and Rebound (1996), which redefined "go anywhere" with its ability to flip over and keep on going. It has become the biggest-selling R/C vehicle ever.

SILLY FUN

Some toys are so bizarre and goofy that they defy categorization. What is a Slinky anyhow? Is a yo-yo a game or a sport? Is a Magic Eight Ball a fun diversion or a predictor of fortunes? Who can say? But one thing is true of all these toys: They are a lighthearted way for your child to have fun and be active. Children enjoy being silly—and what better way to promote joy than through such wacky toys as Mexican jumping beans, Sea Monkeys, Magic Rocks, or Wooly Willy?

While some toys might not seem educational, children can always find ways to learn from their experiences. Great examples of fun toys abound: Beautiful glass marbles offer challenging games that improve dexterity. Products like Silly Putty provide tactile pleasure and the opportunity to develop dexterity. Even novelty magic tricks serve a purpose. They give children a fun way to gain confidence in their ability to anticipate problems and think through solutions.

So don't forget your old childhood favorites, such as jacks, which are one of mine. Having fun doesn't need to make sense, and there are some great nonsensical choices among these selections.

Silly Putty

Silly Putty was a byproduct of a search to find a synthetic substitute for rubber. James Wright, a chemical engineer working for General Electric, came up with the flesh-colored silicone compound that bounced when rolled into a ball and stretched like rubber. Handy for picking up lint and cleaning surfaces, Silly Putty also picked up images off the printed page. Wright dubbed it "Gooey Gup," and he sold it out of a New Haven, Connecticut, toy store. A businessman named Peter Hodgson saw it in 1949 and bought the rights from Wright. He renamed it Silly Putty and enclosed it in a bright red plastic egg and sold it through bookstores. Hodgson sold thirty-two million eggs in five years. In 1988 Binney & Smith began selling it in green, yellow, and blue eggs as well as the original red one.

MR. POTATO HEAD

PLAY WITH YOUR FOOD WITHOUT MAKING A MESS

3–7 years

With its mix-and-match features and goofy expression, Mr. Potato Head teaches children how to create and transform a face—and how to laugh. While having loads of fun, they are developing imagination and language skills. Playing with Mr. Potato Head also helps very young kids determine the proper places for body parts, helping them visualize a face when they attempt to draw on their own.

The early Mr. Potato Head, introduced in 1952 by George Lerner, capitalized on kids' desire to play with their food. He molded twenty-eight features and accessories to fit on an actual potato (not supplied).

Plastic eyes, ears, mouth, mustache, hats, and so on could be added to turn the vegetable into a comic character. In 1953 Mr. Potato Head became the first toy to be advertised on television, and he took a bride—Mrs. Potato Head. By 1964, when Hasbro bought the rights, a plastic potato was supplied. In 1974 Mr. Potato Head doubled in size. After his star turn in the *Toy Story* movies, Mr. Potato Head became the host of his own live-action show on the Fox Family Network. At the turn of the twenty-first century, his popularity shows no signs of slowing.

TIPS TO EXTEND THE LIFE OF YOUR TOYS

1. Rinse off products baby or toddler chews on, using warm, soapy water to wipe off plush toys and diluted, chlorinated water for hard, washable products.
2. Provide plenty of storage areas that are accessible to children.
3. Reduce clutter of toys on the floor, so they won't be easily broken.
4. Remove toys that are not current favorites and reintroduce them later.

HULA HOOP

A HIP-TWISTING CHALLENGE

6 years and up

Hula hoops bring out the competitive spirit in all children. How many times can they spin the hoop on their hips before it slips to the ground? A great exercise, hula hooping helps children release a lot of physical energy, while enabling them to work on their physical skills and improve their coordination. Popular since they were first introduced in 1959, hula hoops continue to offer fun for the whole family.

Wham-O founders Arthur Melin and Richard Knerr saw children in

**BEN ASEN,
THIS BOOK'S PHOTOGRAPHER
CIRCA 1963**

Australia using a bamboo hoop during a school exercise routine. They thought the hoop would catch on with American kids. They introduced it in southern California playgrounds, and its popularity spread. Hula hoops became an immediate fad and sold twenty-five million in the first four months and one hundred million within two years. They were originally made out of wood but were soon switched to plastic. Little plastic pellets were added by Wham-O to give the hoops their characteristic sound.

Hoopla

- In 1987 Roxanne Rose spun a hula hoop for ninety hours at Washington State University.

- The world record for the most people simultaneously hula-hooping was set in 1990 in New Brunswick, Canada, by two thousand people.

- In 1999 Wham-O kicked off a fifty-day coast-to-coast charity drive for the Boys' and Girls' Clubs of America to celebrate fifty years of Wham-O.

SLINKY

AS INEXPENSIVE AS IT IS ENTERTAINING

2–12 years

When taken out of its box, a Slinky is full of activity, surprise, and animation. Looking like a spring from a hardware store, it's a toy that becomes fun once it moves. Children are intrigued by the sound and its ability to flip down the stairs. They will watch it make its way down (teaching them a little about gravity) and then do it over and over again. Slinky is also fun to hold, unravel, and move back and forth. Children never seem to tire of the novelty.

Slinky has been one of the industry's most popular toys since its debut in 1945. Once Richard and Betty James convinced Gimbel Brothers' department store to allow them to display a Slinky walking down a slant board, they sold four hundred Slinkies in an hour.

Slinky's origins are less amazing. Marine engineer Richard James was working in a shipyard when a torsion spring used in the testing meter fell off his desk and jumped end over end across the floor. He took it home and said to his wife, "I think I can make a toy out of this." He devised a steel formula that allowed the spring to walk, and the Jameses set up a small factory. Since its initial response at Gimbel Brothers', more than 250 million Slinkies have been purchased. Betty James said that the explanation for Slinky's success is "its simplicity. That's the way it started." And its affordability helps, too. In 1945 the original Slinky sold for a dollar. Now that same Slinky sells for only $1.99.

It's Fun for a Girl and a Boy

- Eighty feet of wire was used in the original metal Slinky.
- Fifty thousand tons of wire, or three million miles of steel wire, have been used since the toy's first release—enough to go around the earth 126 times.
- The first Slinky television advertisement debuted in 1946 on Miss Patty's *Romper Room*.
- The Slinky's jingle is the longest running in advertising history.

YO-YO

A POCKETFUL OF TRICKS

7 years and up

A yo-yo is a perfect toy for learning skills that involve coordination, balance, eye-hand coordination, and dexterity. Children gain self-confidence and self-esteem as they learn to do tricks with their yo-yos. That is a lot of value for one of the least expensive and most enduring toys around. Yo-yos are perfect for taking along on a trip. They demonstrate gravity and encourage observation, patience, and follow-through. Anyone ready to walk the dog or go around the world?

The yo-yo is an ancient toy that became a modern favorite. In ancient China, yo-yos were made of ivory with satin cords. In ancient Greece, they were made from terra-cotta. A Grecian bowl dating back to 450 B.C. shows the yo-yo. In the seventeenth and eighteenth centuries it became a plaything of the royal courts, decorated with jewels or painted with patterns. There's even evidence that soldiers in Napoleon's army played with yo-yos during battles (and they still won!).

The modern version of the yo-yo had its origins in the South Pacific. The word *yo-yo* means "*come back*" in the Tagalog language of the Philippines. It is believed that in the Philippine Islands, traditional hunters used a version of the yo-yo—a vine around a piece of flint—to kill animals and then easily retrieve the weapon.

In 1927, a Filipino busboy at a hotel in Santa Monica amused the guests by performing tricks with his handcrafted yo-yos. Donald Duncan took notice and offered to buy him out. In 1929 Duncan, who also invented the parking meter, began making wooden yo-yos. He demonstrated them in department stores. They became popular during the depression, then, after a brief lull, Duncan reintroduced yo-yos in flashy new colors and styles, such as a glow-in-the-dark version. This repackaging helped the yo-yo regain its popularity. During the sixties, Duncan produced more than sixty million yo-yos. One of its current incarnations includes flashing lights and electronic noises.

VIEWMASTER 3-D VIEWER

A 3-D GLIMPSE AT THE WONDERS OF THE WORLD

3–7 years

Children enjoy looking at pictures and creating stories to match. For this activity, Viewmaster is the perfect toy. Available in hundreds of themes, Viewmaster is a portable 3-D glimpse at the wonders of the world—stories, places, people, animals, and more. Invented before television became widespread, the viewer remains an exciting way to see and explore.

The Viewmaster was first introduced in 1939 at the New York World's Fair. William Gruber, a piano tuner from Portland, Oregon, had the idea of mass-producing color 3-D images in a viewer. He teamed up with Harold Graves, the president of a local photofinishing and postcard company, to create a portable viewer based on the stereo photograph viewer. When it was introduced at the New York and San Francisco World's Fairs in 1940, Viewmaster was an immediate hit. During World War II, the viewer was used as a training tool by the military. After the war, Sawyer's purchased Tru-Vue, a film-strip company that owned the license to the Disney characters. From then on, Viewmaster became a favorite children's toy. The GAF company took over the product and created the talking Viewmaster, which brought cartoon reels to life. They also made a stereo viewer. Viewmaster is now distributed by the Tyco division of Mattel.

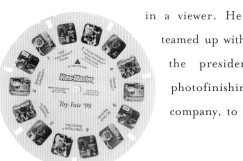

FINGER PUPPETS

FOR ASPIRING YOUNG ACTORS

3-8 years

Puppets are beloved by children and can be very educational. Playing with a finger puppet helps children develop their imagination and language skills and encourages them to express themselves. They enjoy making up shows spontaneously, performing for each other and for a wider audience. This is a great activity to do together as a family and is particularly suited for travel.

Manhattan Toy, who makes wonderful finger puppets, also makes a theater for your puppets that folds up into a convenient carrying case and has handy storage compartments to hold puppets and props. It is fifteen inches tall and offers children a great way to present their shows. The theater is available with four finger puppets, and others can be added. A variety of puppets are offered by Manhattan, including insects, flowers, animals, and royalty.

The Manhattan Toy Company began in 1983 under the creative hand of Francis Goldwyn, the grandson of the famous Hollywood producer Samuel Goldwyn. Francis created Floppies, soft toys that can be hugged or even sat on. Then came the popular Dino line for all ages. In 1990 the company was acquired by Carousel and has since expanded to include Wimmer Ferguson, Pappa Geppetto's, Hoopla by Andre, and other lines, offering a great variety of playthings for babies through older children.

OUTDOOR TOYS

PATHWAYS TO ATHLETIC ADVENTURE

Children need fresh air every day. Outdoor play allows them to explore the natural world and build overall strength and endurance. If you take toys along on every outing, your child will enjoy the outdoors even more—try a pogo stick, moon shoes, or a Frisbee. Or simply take a walk—just getting out of the house is a refreshing change and inspires a lot of discovery.

Outdoor activities provide great exercise—from jumping rope, which promotes coordination, to skating, which encourages graceful movement, to playing with balls or paddles, to riding a bike. In the swelter of summer, many activities can also keep kids cool: running under lawn sprinklers, splashing in backyard pools, swinging on swings. Even snow and cold can't keep kids inside, with skating, sledding, snowshoeing, and skiing tempting them to go outdoors.

Being outside is also a good opportunity for the whole family to play together. Look for a great kite to fly on a windy day, a Frisbee to throw at the beach, and a hula hoop to twirl at a birthday party. Your child will enjoy mastering new skills while spending important time with you.

Outdoor toys are available from Air Pogo, Fisher-Price, Hedstrom, Little Tikes, Step 2, and Today's Kids. Good generic toys include balls, toy boats, pails and shovels, skates, swings, and plastic pools.

TRICYCLE

A CHILD'S FIRST TASTE OF FREEDOM
2–4 years

A bike, no matter what the form, is one of the few real escapes for a child. While every other element of their lives may be scheduled and chauffeured, children are free when they ride their bikes. And nothing is better than a Roadmaster Tricycle to introduce a child to the open road. With double-dipped paint and beautiful chrome handlebars, this deluxe tricycle even looks fast.

As high as it is wide, the Roadmaster is hard to topple and, with an all-steel frame and seat, even harder to damage. The unique powder-coat paint process adds luster and shine and also makes it easy to find amid the flotsam and jetsam on the market. Now marketed under the Flexible Flyer name, this bike will always hold a special place in your child's heart.

· TOYS I REMEMBER ·

Fighting Lady, an ersatz battleship that you played with on the floor, had a cannon on her forward deck, torpedo tubes mid-hip, and battery-operated lights and horns—all the tools need to recreate Victory at Sea. *I remember the ads on television, which I'd see after returning home from school in the afternoon, and the immediate, overwhelming desire to have it for Christmas. The hours playing with her both expressed and deepened my fascination with all things military and, in due course, with the history that gives those things context. The line from that toy boat to my role as president of* American Heritage *may not be simple and direct, but it is surely real.*
— TIM FORBES, president of *American Heritage*

BIG BALL HOPPER

A LITTLE BOUNCING IMPROVES BALANCE

5–8 years

Children like to play with this item for a couple of reasons. The hopping itself is a fun way for children to improve balance and coordination while developing their gross motor skills. And while this type of toy has been available for years, the bing balls inside the Hedstrom version of the hopper now provide the child with the additional payoff of a wacky sound. Hedstrom has produced standard balls and play balls that are ten, fourteen, and eighteen inches in diameter. The popularity of these toys led to the development of the Sound Hop, which has a computer chip that activates three different sounds depending on the child's bouncing action.

In 1914 Eagle Rubber started manufacturing rubber toy balloons. In 1923 rubber and sponge balls were introduced and Eagle expanded, eventually being bought by Hedstrom. In 1991 Ditri Associates (the present management) purchased the Hedstrom Corporation, continuing its reputation for quality.

108

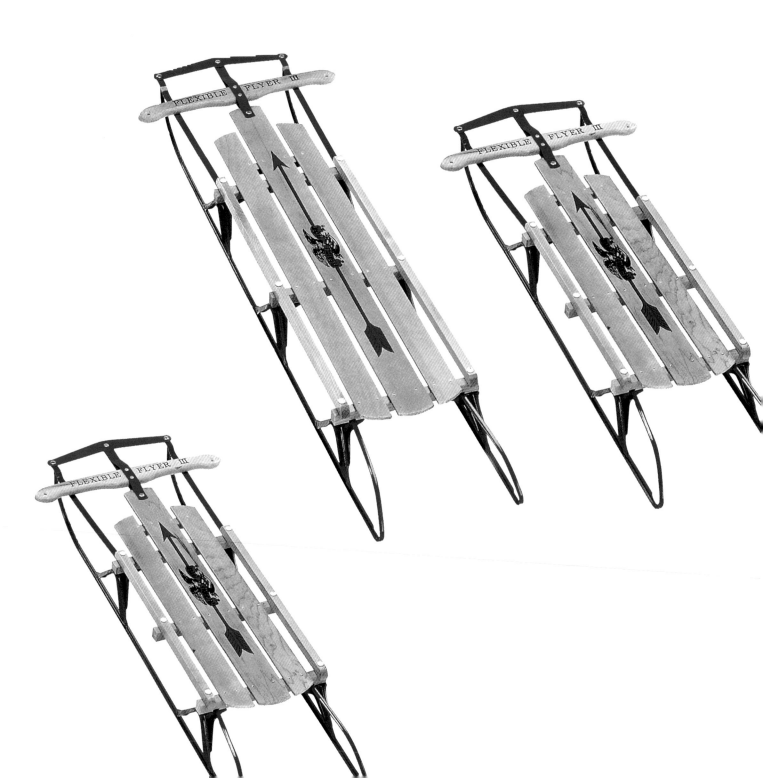

FLEXIBLE FLYER SLED

GREAT FOR GETTING OUTSIDE IN WINTER

7 years and up

A great way to celebrate the change of seasons is to take a sled out on a snowy day and slide down a hill. The enjoyment only grows as you trudge up the hill and repeat the process over and over. Sledding is one of life's most memorable activities for children who have access to snowy conditions.

The Flexible Flyer is a wonderful sled, largely due to its extraordinary craftsmanship. Your child will have a smooth ride on rust-resistant runners. The sled handles superbly as it glides down the hill, due to its patented steering bar. Made from American hardwood and steel with a unique no-flake powder-coat paint process, the Flyer has a durable construction made for years of enjoyment.

Motivated by the need to keep his farm factory employees busy year-round, Samuel Leeds Allen looked for a product that could be made in the fall and sold for the winter—a sled! In 1889 he devised a beauty, with flexible steel and a movable, steerable crossbar. After five years of flagging sales, the Flexible Flyer finally caught on, becoming an icon of fun that is still cherished more than a century later.

CLASSIC RED WAGON

A CLASSIC CARRY-ALL

18 months—10 years

What could be more fun to use outdoors than this basic red wagon? First introduced in 1933, the Radio Flyer is the ultimate vehicle of a child's imagination. Children turn wagons into cars, trains, stagecoaches, battleships, doll carriages, forts, and sandboxes. Anything that can be loaded up or moved around will eventually find its way into the wagon.

In 1917 Anton Pasin, a craftsman who built furniture and cabinets, began making handcrafted wagons in his workshop. By 1930 his company, Radio Steel and Manufacturing, was the largest producer of coaster wagons. In 1933, sixteen years after the company's founding, he built the forty-five-foot-tall Coastery Boy exhibit that was the hit of the Chicago World's Fair.

For his now-classic metal wagon he chose two evocative names: *Radio* because the medium was in its heyday and to honor fellow Italian inventor Guglielmo Marconi; and *Flyer*, which recognized the wonder of flight. The Radio Flyer red paint is custom-mixed using a special formula that is a closely guarded secret. To celebrate the company's eightieth anniversary in 1997, the company renamed itself Radio Flyer and created the world's largest wagon: twenty-seven feet long and thirteen feet wide—nine times the size of the original wagon. The company is owned by the Pasin family.

FAO SCHWARZ, 1973

FRISBEE

AFFORDABLE, PORTABLE FUN

5 years and up

Throwing a Frisbee can be great exercise for lots of people at once. Inexpensive and extremely portable, it is the perfect game for picnics and other family gatherings when you want everyone to get in the act and have fun together.

The idea for the Frisbee came from a metal pie tin originally manufactured by the Frisbee Baking Company of Bridgeport, Connecticut. During the 1920s, students at nearby Yale University threw the tins around for fun and yelled "Frisbee," to warn passersby. Fred Morrison, a carpenter and building inspector who was fascinated with flight and plastic, came up with the design for a flying disc. Wham-O bought the idea and named it Pluto Power, because it resembled a flying saucer. In 1957 Wham-O modified the plastic disc and trademarked the name Frisbee. Frisbee-throwing became a popular activity to do at picnics, at the beach, or even at organized championships. One version that became very popular glowed in the dark. Since its debut, Wham-O has produced more than one hundred million discs.

Frisbee Fun!

- In 1998 a man from Colorado threw a disc more than 690 feet to set a world distance record.
- In 1957 the first international Frisbee tournament was held in Escanaba, Michigan.
- In 1963 the U.S. Navy tested Frisbees as a way to keep flares aloft.
- In 1967 the International Frisbee Association was founded.

NERF BALLS

YOU *CAN* PLAY BALL IN THE HOUSE

6 years and up

The parental warning, "Don't play ball in the house," was the inspiration for the Nerf. Perfect for both indoors and out, this fun and inexpensive ball helps children gain physical skill, dexterity, and flexibility. Because they are so easy to grasp, Nerf balls improve coordination and physical confidence. They can provide hours of fun, especially in inclement weather when children are confined indoors. The balls come in many different types, so you can find the right ball to fit your child's ability and age.

In addition to Nerf balls, Hasbro makes Nerf versions of many classic outdoor toys, including basketball and baseball sets, darts, and the world's best-selling football. A popular addition to traditional sports toys is the soft pellet gun which offers a safe way to play rough. Three popular products are Secret Shot, Triple Strikes, and Glider Launcher.

In 1970 Twister inventor Reyn Guyer decided to capitalize on his success and started a game-development company. While creating a caveman game with foam rocks, Guyer realized that he was on to something. With a foam ball, you could play all of the traditional outdoor activities without anyone getting hurt or anything getting broken. He showed the concept to Parker Brothers, who gave the name *Nerf* to the first official indoor ball. Parker Brothers is now owned by Hasbro.

KOOSH BALLS

FOR A CHILD'S FIRST GAME OF CATCH

3 years and up

For a toy that looks something like a porcupine, the Koosh ball is surprisingly soft and easy to throw, which inspires confidence in kids of all ages. Its unique construction makes dropping it virtually impossible. The company has developed soft and safe products that stimulate children's imaginations and promote healthy, interactive play. The Koosh's success led to the development of sports sets— such as darts, paddleball, and hoops—that make active play safer and even let children play indoors.

In 1986 Scott Stillinger was frustrated by not having a safe ball to help teach his children to catch. He saw that most balls rolled away too easily. He designed the Koosh ball, a mass of radiating rubber filaments, and a star was born.

Oddz On is now part of the Hasbro family.

· TOYS I REMEMBER ·

Much of my childhood was spent playing with one of the finest toys ever devised—a Meccano set (I believe Erector is the U.S. equivalent). But Erector is far more than a toy—it trained several generations of engineers, giving them the feel of metal. I'm terrified that today's computer-trained engineers will lack this vital skill—with disastrous results!

—ARTHUR C. CLARKE, author of *2001: A Space Odyssey*

FUTURE
TOYS

Looking toward the millennium and beyond, what is the future of toys?

While there have always been interactive toys, from wind-ups to moving kites to delightful music boxes, recent advances in electronics have taken toys to a whole new level. Now even our old favorites have been transformed and made new. For example:

- The yo-yo has been modernized to include sounds, lights, and even the ability to measure the number of rotations and speed.
- Dolls, once quiet and passive, can now wriggle and talk and have vocabularies of up to ten thousand words.
- Games that used to be played by two or three around a table can now be played on a computer—between game machines or against another person who is plugged into the TV or by computer through the Internet.

Today's toys interact—they don't just sit there waiting for a child to make them move. They shake, tickle, talk, walk, and respond to voice and touch. Some toys can talk to each other in a language that is all their own. A few toys will even complain or "die" if not cared for properly (a huge responsibility).

While technology has extended toys' capabilities, they still require the child to be involved. Children do respond to software at an early age, enjoying the colors and shapes, watching movements, and hearing sounds. Electronics has revolutionized playtime. But critics caution that such programs should be used only when the child is ready and then only for limited amounts of time. Moving a mouse around is no substitute for drawing a picture or building a skyscraper of blocks.

The MIT Media Laboratory's Toys of Tomorrow Project studies the manner in which high technology and computers have revolutionized the way kids play. The idea behind the MIT project is to let children take more creative control of their games. Mitch Resnick, who heads Toys of Tomorrow's Epistemology

and Learning Group, explains how technology changes the way children learn: "Whoever is doing the inventing is doing most of the learning." He says, "With traditional bricks you can build models of buildings, which makes you think about how buildings stand up or why buildings sometimes fall down. But with traditional blocks you couldn't build a model of an active rabbit. Now kids can build a model of a rabbit, which makes them start thinking about how animals behave."

With modern tools, children can begin to think beyond the square. For example, one pet project at MIT is a green fluffy bug who imitates body movements by picking them up through an antennae-equipped sensor strapped to its back. The toy can sense the movements and even the mood of its owner—less of a thing and more of a creature that knows you and knows your habits.

High-tech toys can help kids grow and learn in ways traditional toys can't. Children can choose between open-ended play with blocks and directed activities on a computer. Today children have an unprecedented range of opportunities—and tomorrow they will have even more.

HANDHELD TOYS

Handheld, cartridge-based gaming systems include animation, sound, and music and the touch-screen interface. They have backlit screens and built-in software, and they offer a variety of different games like Sonic Jam, racing, wrestling, and Frogger, plus interactive versions of traditional games such as Scrabble and Monopoly. In general, these games increase fine motor skills and allow children to become comfortable and confident using current technology.

Nintendo's Gameboy offers many titles, including a new and popular game, Pokémon, in which the goal is to find, capture, and train various monsters, all in an effort to become the world's greatest Pokémon trainer. There are more than

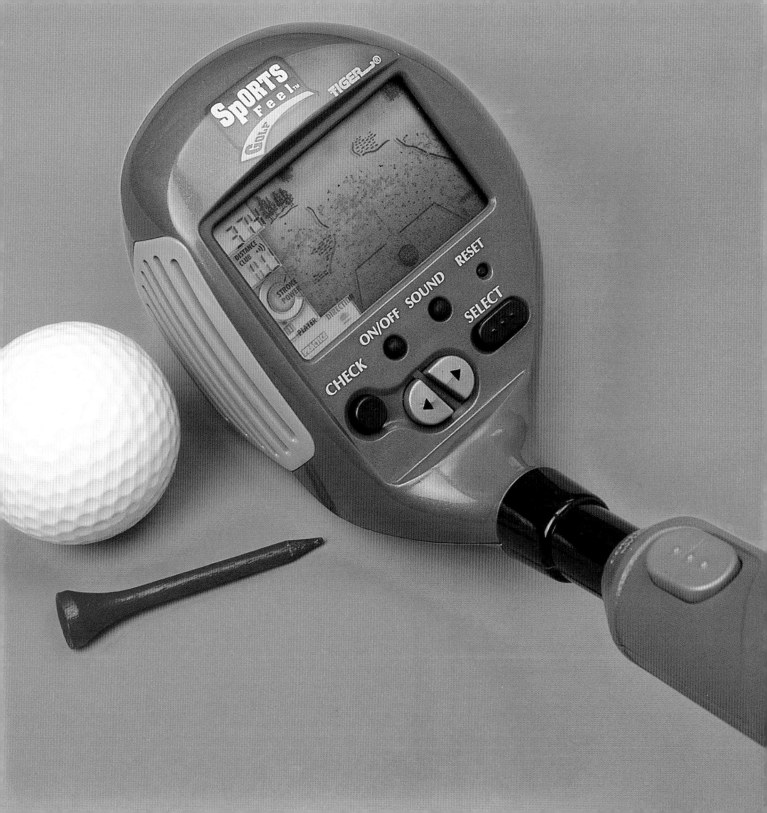

150 Pokémon, including the cute Pikachu, who appeals to both girls and boys because he is cuddly and able to fight. Other titles include Frogger, Tetris, and A Bug's Life.

There are handheld light-and-sound games that respond electronically. Pro Drag Racing by Parker Brothers has realistic sounds and vibration; you'll feel like you're in the cockpit of a nitro-powered dragster. Sports Feel Golf by Tiger enables you to choose your club, get into stance, and actually swing the club to hit the ball.

For smaller children, there is a variety of games that increase a child's understanding of cause and effect and offer tactile, visual, and auditory stimulation. Rugrats Hot Potato is a hide-and-seek game that tests memory skills, and VTECH's Tiny Touch Phone Plus stimulates self-discovery and strengthens fine motor skills.

Tamagotchi is another popular interactive toy that can be worn around the neck of a child. When the game is activated, the little egg on the screen becomes a chick that has all of the animal's real needs, including eating, sleeping, and playing. Tamagotchis make great learning tools because they require a high level of responsibility.

• • •

PRE-COMPUTERS

Not only in school but in life, children need to understand how to use computers as a tool for success. Luckily, the toy industry helps fulfill these needs by continuously translating technology into products that will benefit children. Through a combination of content, game play, and design, manufacturers and inventors have changed the way that children learn.

Remember our old friend Pooh Bear? Well, he's evolved to fit today's child of the future. Now there is Pooh ABC Smart Stick by Tiger, an electronic learning aide that can identify voices, colors, fruits, and vegetables, increasing word-image association with engaging animation. The characters' voices encourage a child's response.

VTECH created Little Miss LapTop for girls entering school, with twenty-four activities that introduce letters, spelling, math, logic, music, and games. Designed to help the child learn basic computer skills, this laptop has a realistic keyboard, mouse, and LCD screen.

According to Dennis Burke, the president of Team Concepts, North American Division, "The computer will be a way of life for our children and generations that follow." A great product from this company, for children ages five through seven, is the ComQuest Disk Master. This dazzling electronic talking computer has thirty fun activities on a laptop-type system. It's designed to help kids get comfortable with computers while stimulating learning in subjects like music, time, letters/words, numbers, and strategy. For older children there is a Web-Start computer that enables children to test out the Internet. Learning activities are designed like the real Web, with an e-mail Web Page Creator, geography,

geometry, vocabulary puzzles, games, dictionary, and a sign-off and enter password.

Another forward-thinking company is Leap Frog. Its goal is to provide interactive learning materials to help children understand phonics, reading, math, science, geography, and space. One of its products, Book Wizard, brings traditional paper books to life. When children touch any point on a page with a pen, they will hear the story, the pronunciation of words, the phonics sounds of letters, the names of objects, and other sounds. Mike Wood, founder and CEO of Leap Frog, predicts that "innovative near-touch technology will revolutionize the way people learn."

That technology is also used in two other Leap Frog products, Explorer and Odyssey, which are globes that offer games to make learning geography fun. Children can learn the names of countries, play national anthems, measure the distance between two places, and give local times and other information. There are ten thousand facts built into

each globe about a country's culture, economics, religion, music, and more.

Educational Insights, whose goal is to build young minds and encourage fun and learning, offers a wide array of electronic products. Two award-winning toys are GeoSafari and GeoSafari Jr. These fun-filled electronic learning systems guide and reward one or more students through fascinating full-color, educator-written lessons in geography, learning basics, history, science, animals, puzzles, thinking games, sports, languages, and much more. Easy, flexible programming keeps games competitive among students of different skill levels.

• • •

INTELLITOYS

The first Intellitoy was Teddy Ruxpin, an automatic responding bear who could read books aloud. When he was introduced in 1987, he took the toy industry by storm. His success spawned countless imitators and innovators.

When Tickle Me Elmo hit stores in 1998, he caused Christmas-shopping hordes to triple in size. Who wouldn't want this friendly Sesame Street character, whose giggles and shakes made everybody laugh? Elmo was the ideal character to launch a line of plush toys that reacted to a child's touch. A recent Sesame Street edition is Yum Yum Cookie Monster, who does exactly what you'd expect—he eats lots of cookies!

Another variation on the plush learning toy is the ActiMate, a doll that interacts with children in response to touch. According to Dr. Eric Strommen, the developmental psychologist and designer for Microsoft, ActiMates Interactive Teletubbies help children get a head start on learning vocabulary and distinguishing sights, sounds, and colors in ways that are both fun and educational. Teletubbies also have ActiMates TV pack, which links with coded Teletubbies videos and TV broadcasts. ActiMates have been created around other TV characters too, including Barney, Arthur, and D.W.

Another popular Intellitoy is Furby. Inventor Dave Hampton told *Time* magazine that the toy's creation had been inspired by the wonder he felt caring for his childhood pet, an iguana named Iggy. "Living things have incredible depth to them," says Hampton. "Children appreciate that. They're excited by it. I'd like to see new toys that approach that level of depth and richness, and I think we can do that with computers."

Children are able to learn vocabulary and skills by watching and interacting with this furry, funny, Animatronic pet. Furby interacts with his environment through sight, touch, hearing, and location. His eyes open and close, his ears wiggle, his mouth moves, and he can move and dance on a small foot. Each Furby is intelligent and able to learn. First he will tell you his name. He will speak to you in his own language, "Furbish." He will begin to learn English and communicate using English words. His vocabulary of two hundred words is 40 percent Furbish, 40 percent English, and 20 percent sounds. He is able to say more than eight hundred phrases. Ultimately, by using Furbish and English, he will be able to communicate. He is also sensitive to his environment and will react to stimuli. This Intellitoy is more than a toy, less than a pet, and more like a friend.

• • •

DIGITAL BUILDING BLOCKS

While children gain a wide variety of benefits through traditional building blocks, innovations in the industry have led to the creation of unique building sets that push the envelope of shape and form. These sets focus on eye-hand coordination, increasing social skills, thinking abstractly, planning ahead, and testing children's imagination and ability.

For children ages two and up, Neurosmith has created Music Blocks, a toy that enables children to create their own musical masterpieces simply by playing with blocks. The music is activated by placing the blocks at random or by design according to the shapes on the sides of the blocks and their colors.

Music Blocks comes with five blocks, a Mozart's Night Music cartridge, and a comprehensive guide for parents titled "Music and Your Child's Mind."

Lucas Learning Ltd., a company committed to creating uncommon learning experiences through software, creates games that are imaginative, challenging, and engaging, yet grounded in solid content and with an understanding of how children actually learn. For example, their *Star Wars* DroidWorks, designed for children ages ten and up, is a unique combination of construction set and adventure game that enables children to learn and apply scientific principles. As an undercover Rebel agent deep within the Jawa Droid Workshop on Tatooine, children must design and build droids with unique attributes to complete a series of missions.

Lego, the king of building blocks, has invested over a decade of research with MIT to create Mindstorms. The Robotics Invention System—the core set of the Lego Mindstorms—lets children design and program real robots that do what they want them to. Children can create everything from a light-sensitive intruder alarm to a robotic rover that can follow a trail, move around obstacles, and duck into dark corners. The heart of the Robotics Invention System is the RCX, an autonomous Lego microcomputer that can be programmed using a PC. The RCX serves as the brain of Lego Mindstorms inventions. Children first build their robot using the RCX and more than seven hundred pieces, attaching sensors, motors, gears, and other Lego bricks. Then they create a program for their invention using RCX Code, a simple, powerful programming language. Next they can download their program to the RCX using a special infrared transmitter. Their creation can now interact with the environment, fully autonomous from the computer.

Rokenbok is an expandable building system that allows your children to build and then control their creations through radio control. All of the Rokenbok sets have interchangeable pieces. After purchasing a Start Set, which contains the central Command Deck, children can expand their system any way they choose. Building sets include Bridge, Roadway, and

Construction sets, and accessories sets include a Conveyor and a Down-a-Vator.

. . .

SCIENCE TOYS

Wild Planet, an innovative company, creates products that kids find cool. Real gear, detailed gadgets, and the ultimate spy tools inspire kids to go beyond the ordinary. From the cryogenic lab Ice Man to the experiment chamber MegaDome, Wild Planet stands for innovation, quality, and positive experiences for children. One of its toys is an electronic learning device called Super Sonic Ear, which magnifies sounds, allowing children to listen to birds, insects, and other sounds in their environment. Another is a pair of Spy Camera sunglasses that allow children to take pictures of what they see without anyone knowing. With these toys at their command, children are limited only by their imagination.

Kits that explain scientific principles are always a welcome addition to toy shelves. Educational Designs has a variety of labs to help children explore natural phenomena. Electrolab, for children seven and up, enables children to build a motor and a motor boat, a crystal radio, and a bell buzzer, all while learning about electricity. In the Earth, Sun, and Sky Lab, children learn about geology, solar energy, and aerodynamics in the three-in-one kit. Human and animal biology is explained through a series of kits by Skilcraft, including Insectlab, Dinolab, and Life Cell Lab, which enable children to grow yeast cells and see how they function. Wild Goose bases its kits on famous scientists' discoveries. For example, Newton's Greatest Hits uses springs, ball bearings, roller coasters, and a mathematical teeter-totter to explain Newton's Laws.

. . .

PC TOYS

Playtime can be a "plug-in" adventure if your child is ready to benefit from and enjoy new technology. Games, software, and CD-ROMs can combine to become a virtual schoolhouse, making

learning dramatic and fun while introducing and familiarizing youngsters with computers and their capabilities.

Children as young as eighteen months can begin exploring a cyber environment. One title, Reader Rabbit's Toddler by the Learning Company, uses the background of a magic garden to explore a variety of early skills, including learning the alphabet, counting to five, identifying shapes and colors, matching, improving early vocabulary, recognizing sounds and listening patterns, developing memory skills, mouse control, following directions, and learning music, songs, and rhymes.

Knowledge Adventure distributes the JumpStart Home Learning System, a complete suite of educational software for elementary school children ages four through eleven. A perfect home learning supplement, the JumpStart Home Learning System includes a comprehensive library of twelve award-winning, best-selling JumpStart grade-and-subject-specific CD-ROMs, from kindergarten through fifth grade—plus value-added academic assessment software and supplemental activity workbooks.

Microsoft and Scholastic have teamed up to produce wonderful educational software based on the award-winning book series *The Magic School Bus*, by Joanna Cole and Bruce Degen, which features a wacky science teacher named Ms. Frizzle, who takes her class of enthusiastic, inquisitive students and playful sidekick, Liz the lizard, on educational field trips in her magically transformable bus. In separate CD-ROMs the crazy crew explores the ocean, dinosaurs, the solar system, the Earth's core, the rain forest, and animals. In one CD-ROM, *Magic School Bus Explores the Human Body*, human biology comes to life with narration, sound, video, and animation—plus games, experiments, and reports.

Mattel and Intel have joined forces to create products that combine the power of PCs and the magic of toys into a new generation of interactive play. Two products, Intel Play X3 Microscope (with which children can magnify and display microscopic objects on their PC screens and then play with the images in creative ways) and Intel Play Me2Cam (with which children see themselves on the computer screen and use their own bodies to navigate in a virtual world) apply technology in imaginative ways to create never-seen-before play experiences.

Kids get the hands-on experience of a toy and the magic of multimedia software in one with Tonka Workshop CD-ROM Playsets, Hasbro Interactive's first title in the interactive-toy category. Tonka Workshop empowers children to create, build, and play the Tonka way—while providing an easy-to-use, no-tech interface with a cool Tonka tool set and a super-fun CD-ROM. In Tonka Workshop, kids use six durable plastic tools contained in a key-top playset to build projects, play exciting tool games, and com-

plete repair jobs around Tonka town.

The wealth of software titles, from home reference to classic games to school-based subjects, is staggering. The titles described here are proven award-winners from companies you can trust, but they do not even scratch the surface of what is available. Parents should keep in mind the following criteria when purchasing software for their child: Is it easy to understand and explore? Does it give a positive response for correct answers and explain the reason for a negative response? Does it have good graphics, sound, and animation? Is it appropriate for your child's developmental needs? Is it fun and enjoyable for the child? If the answer to these questions is "yes," then this software is probably appropriate.

ABOUT DR. TOY

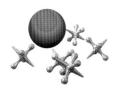

DR. STEVANNE AUERBACH, also known as Dr. Toy, is an expert in play, toys, and children's products as well as in child development and early education. A native New Yorker, she loves visiting FAO with her grandson and watching his reaction to toys.

Dr. Auerbach produces *Dr. Toy's Guide*—the first on-line magazine (www.drtoy.com) to report on toys and children's products. The site contains the reports based on her annual awards, Dr. Toy's Best 100 Children's Products, in which she selects and evaluates the best child development toys and other accoutrements. Additional features include Best Classic Toys and Best Vacation Products.

Dr. Auerbach, the director of the Institute for Childhood Resources in San Francisco, is the author of more than a dozen books, including *Dr. Toy's Smart Play: How to Raise a Child with a High P.Q. (Play Quotient)*, published by St. Martin's Press. "Dr. Toy," her weekly column for King Features Syndicate, appears in newspapers throughout the United States and Canada.

Dr. Auerbach is a consultant and speaker on play and parent-child relationships. She is a member of the National Association for the Education of Young Children (NAEYC), the American Society of Journalists and Authors (ASJA), Women in Toys (WIT), and the American Specialty Toy Retailing Association (ASTRA).

ACKNOWLEDGMENTS

The author wishes to acknowledge the unique participation of several people in this endeavor: the imagination of Byron Preiss; the support of David Niggli, Brooke Adkins, and Lucy Conrad at FAO Schwarz; the dedication and attention to detail of the project editor, Dinah Dunn; the talent of Literary Agent Supreme Laurie Harper (Sebastian Literary Agency); the playfulness and support of Ralph Whitten and Jeff Dunan; the efficient word processing of Carol Niehus and Winifred Stone; the wonderful design of 27.12; the amazing skill of photographer Ben Asen; and the additional help from J. Vita, Timothy Steger, Kathy Huck, and Ruth Ashby. Plus my gratitude goes out to everyone at each of the toy companies who responded so generously to our requests.

This book is dedicated to Josiah and all children who now benefit from the legacy of toys and the growing awareness of the importance of play around the world.

A FINAL THOUGHT FROM FAO SCHWARZ

Founded in 1862, FAO Schwarz has long been the nation's premier specialty toy retailer. Since that time, we have brought smiles to generations of children, always keeping safety and quality as top priorities and focus.

Toys are an integral and fun way for children to learn and grow. Toys help teach children many skills, including eye-hand coordination, color recognition, letters and numbers, as well as important lessons like sharing and communicating.

The toys featured in this book are just a sampling of the dozens of creative and imaginative choices found in every category. Each one has its own unique play value and interest. In the end, it is the toy you remember most fondly from your childhood or the one most treasured by your child that are truly special and unforgettable—toys for a lifetime.

CREDITS

Crayola Crayons and Silly Putty are registered trademarks of Binny & Smith Inc. • Flexible Flyer is a registered trademark of Flexible Flyer • Barbie, Hot Wheels, Frisbee, and Cabbage Patch are registered trademarks of Mattel.• Gymini is a registered trademark of MAYA Group/Tiny Love • Colorforms and the Colorforms logo are registered trademarks of University Games Corporation • Corn Popper, Tap 'n' Turn Bench, and Stacking Rings are registered trademarks of Fisher-Price • Activity Clown and BRIO are registered trademarks of BRIO Corporation • Lionel is a registered trademark of Lionel LLC. Train courtesy of Howell Schechter • Matchbox is a registered trademark of Matchbox International, Ltd. • Lego is a registered trademark of Interlego AG • Duncan is a registered trademark of Duncan Toys Co. • Etch-A-Sketch is a registered trademark of Ohio Arts Company • View-Master and Magna Doodle are registered trademarks of Tyco Industries, Inc. • Mr. Potato Head, Raggedy Ann and Andy, Spirograph, Tinkertoy, Tonka, Candy Land, Chutes and Ladders, Pictionary, Scrabble, Sorry!, G.I. Joe, Lincoln Logs, Monopoly, Play-Doh, Tonka, and Nerf are trademarks of Hasbro, Inc. • Snuffles is a trademark of Gund Inc. • Skwish is a registered trademark of Pappa Geppetto Toys • Steiff is a registered trademark of Steiff USA • Super-Sonic Ear is a registered trademark of Wild Planet Toys • Toobers & Zots is a registered trademark of Hands On Toys, Inc. • Slinky is a registered trademark of James Industries • Playmobil is a registered trademark of Playmobil Inc. • ActiMates is a registered trademark of Microsoft Inc. • Koosh is a registered trademark of OddzOn Toys • Little Smart and VTECH are registered trademarks of VTECH • GeoSafari is a registered trademark of Educational Insights • Gazoobo is a registered trademark of Chicco • Radio Flyer is a registered trademark of Radio Flyer Inc. • Teletubbies is a registered trademark of Ragdoll Productions Ltd.